THE
PIE ROOM

THE PIE ROOM

Calum Franklin

BLOOMSBURY ABSOLUTE
LONDON • OXFORD • NEW YORK • NEW DELHI • SYDNEY

For my wonderful wife Shenali and my family:
I think Dad would have liked this.

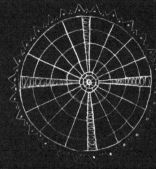

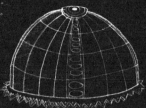

WHITELEYS ART DECO
ROOF SKETCHES
2018

PIE DETAIL
JULY 2017

BEET
WELLINGTON
2019

design for
coronation chicken
pie 15.09.18

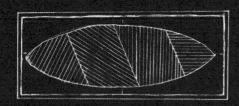

RHUBARB DETAIL
FEB 2018

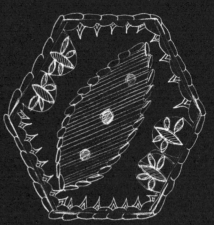

INTRODUCTION

GOOSE PIE DETAILS
DECEMBER
2018

COVENT GARDEN PIE
APRIL 2018

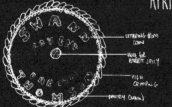

LETTERING FROM COIN

HOLE FOR RABBIT JELLY

HIGH CRIMPING

PASTRY CHAIN

RUHLMAN
PASTRY
DOUGH
BAKED TILL DARK

Introduction

There is a copper-coloured light that spills onto the street in the darkness of night on High Holborn. It falls from The Pie Room, a Victorian kitchen that nestles, like the smallest part in the heart of a Russian doll, into Holborn Dining Room, a grand British brasserie and the main restaurant of one of London's most majestic examples of Edwardian Baroque architecture, the Rosewood London.

It is a room made of marble, brass and copper, which houses chefs hand-crafting hundreds of pieces of savoury pastry a day with jazz and soul music playing gently in the background. It is a room dominated by detail and artistry, that reflects the work happening within. It is a celebration of a constant in British food culture stretching back 600 years and it is where we try to make the most beautiful pies in the land.

To explain how The Pie Room came about, we need to go back a little bit. I was raised in a bakery, child to two of Europe's greatest bakers, often perched on a vast bag of flour while watching them work, scribbling notes from the age of two, studying the mastery, learning the way of the dough.

None of that is true. The reality is that I was raised in South East London by two lovely parents (not bakers) with my two brothers, and my food experience as a child was similar to most British kids in the '80s and '90s; I wasn't foraging for herbs, more foraging for chicken nuggets. But then as I was finishing school I was still unsure of what I wanted to do with my life, and I took a job as a dishwasher at a local restaurant and found my future home immediately in the kitchen. I knew it was an environment where my fidgety energy, not really suitable for desk work, could be channelled to make something of myself.

I worked my way through kitchens, mostly focused on modern European fine dining, learning how to cook properly and to stand up straight. Yes, there were lots of dots of multi-coloured purees and sometimes overly fancy presentations in that style, but the basis of it was really quite old-fashioned, classical cookery … braises, confits, fine pastry work, stocks and sauces. I still use those techniques every day now, but as I got older, I leaned towards a more simple style of cookery, and as indigenous ingredients improved in the country and became more prevalent, I wanted to work more with those and to embrace the roots and history of British cooking. Embracing your own food culture after years and years of cooking others' is liberating, and knowing you can play a little part in improving its reputation is exciting. When Holborn Dining Room arrived, I knew I had a chance to do exactly that.

We opened Holborn Dining Room in early 2014 with a goal to serve the best British produce available, cooked simply in elegant surroundings with service to match. It was a considerable restaurant, seating 180 inside and 50 outside, open all day from early in the morning and with a huge gin selection at the bar. The building it lies within dates back to 1912 and in the deepest basement is a vast equipment store that I was once rummaging through and stumbled upon an antique tin. At first inspection I had no idea what it was for, let alone what era it was from. It turned out to be a complex pie tin with interlocking parts and keys and it intrigued me. I took it up to the main kitchen and asked my chefs if they had ever used one before and quickly realised that I had identified a gap in our knowledge.

With little to reference against we practised using the tin methodically, noting down steps that worked, cooking times and temperatures until finally we thought we had produced something of a high enough standard to make the menu; it took us almost a year of trials to get it right.

That first pie was the beginning of something here, a fascination with lost skills, a revival of handcraft and technique left behind. It reminded me of how much I enjoyed any fine pastry work when I was training; cooking that sometimes felt like small projects because of the skills and discipline needed to get the perfect results.

In the restaurant I started to add more savoury pastry dishes, beef wellingtons, pies and tarts to the menu; they were always well received by our guests and the demand kept building. I wanted a whole pie menu, a celebration of classic British pies and some of our own creations, and our guests wanted it too, but to achieve that and maintain the standard that I look for, we needed to build a special kitchen and the seed was sown for The Pie Room.

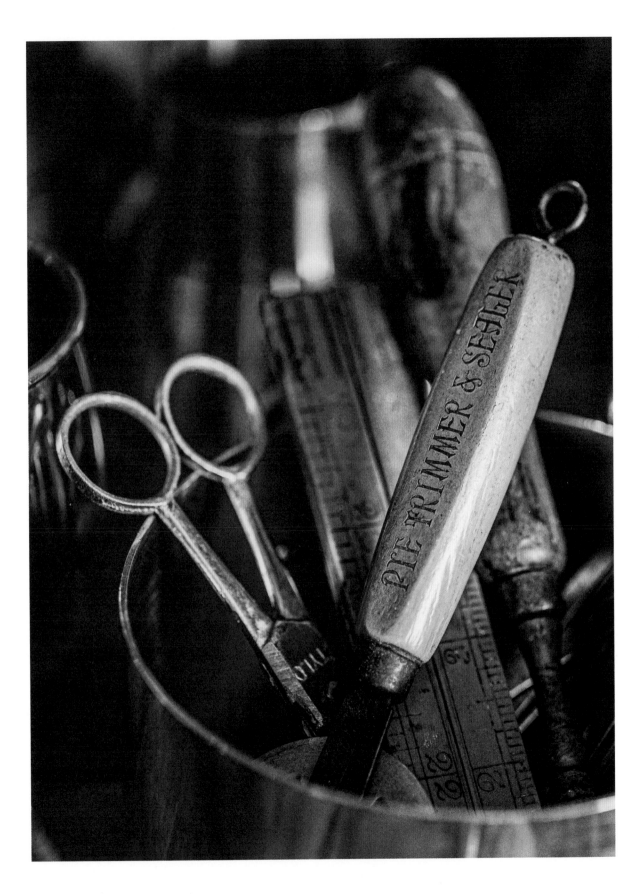

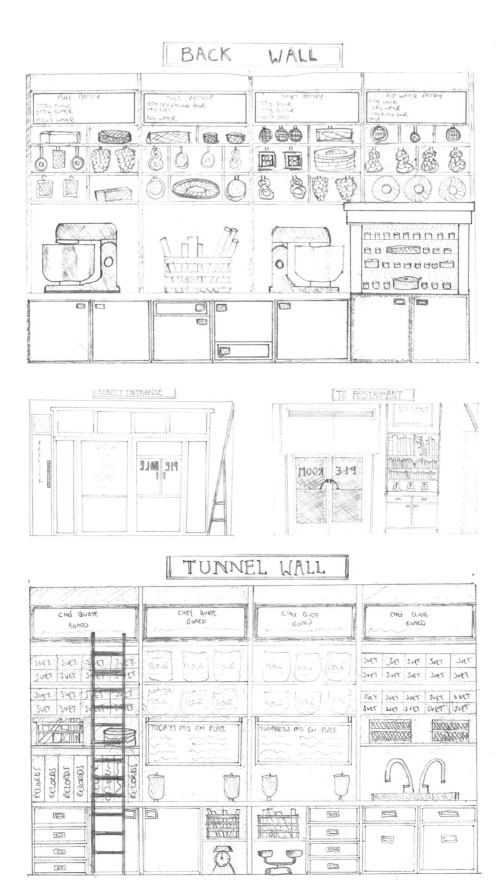

I wanted the room to be a window into the elegant, detailed pastry work that was happening in the restaurant. Its location on the side of the dining room allowed a glass front to the street into which we incorporated hatches through which more homely, rustic pies could be passed at lunchtime when the dining room was full. The Pie Room became a catalyst for change within the restaurant, consolidating its London heritage alongside the Gin Bar and giving Holborn Dining Room a sense of place.

The room took a full year to build because I had drawn the designs by hand. I had a clear vision of how it would be composed, one that was a little tricky, and I was overly stubborn, refusing to compromise on any details ... but it was worth the wait and I'm forever grateful (and sorry!) to all who played a part in its construction; I hope they all look at it now with the same pride that I do.

I've always been a bit weird; I doodle obsessively and always have, usually patterns over and over like Roy and his sculptures in *Close Encounters of the Third Kind*, so design has always been important to me and I've always appreciated the opportunity to create. This room gave me and the team a chance to carve out our little corner in British food history.

The mix of styles of pastry work in the room, from the simple to the extravagant, led to this book. I wanted to share recipes that could be recreated at home by anyone, not just chefs with specialist equipment. I wanted to bring British savoury pastry to a wider audience. The recipes in this book range from dishes that can be made in an evening such as the venison, bone marrow and suet pie, to larger, more celebratory and showstopping work such as the coronation chicken pie. I've also included details on the techniques and skills needed to make your pies as elaborate and beautiful as you wish, and that is exactly where I would start: take your time to work through the information as there are the tools within to make the pastry work achievable at home.

This book is here to remove some of the fear that surrounds pastry work, to build confidence with instructions that make sense in a home kitchen, and to bring The Pie Room direct to you.

TOOLS & TECHNIQUES

EXOPAT

MATFER

Egg Washing

When I first started baking seriously, I would egg wash pies and pastries repeatedly, over and over before baking, to get the best finish possible. Over the years I have realised that in doing so I was wasting not only my time but also that of my kitchen team. Really, the maximum number of times you need to egg wash pastry before baking is twice: this is just as effective as doing it fifteen times.

I use egg yolk mixed with a tiny bit of water – 1 teaspoon of water to 1 egg yolk – and always make sure that the yolk is completely separated from the white, otherwise the finish will be streaky. I pass egg yolks through a fine sieve to remove the chalazae (the white stringy anchors) attached to the yolk.

Egg washing a pie is, in principle, similar to painting a room in your home. You should apply a thin, even coat first and then let it dry before applying the second coat to finish. Between the first and second egg washes, put the pastry in the refrigerator for 20 minutes, while you have a cup of tea and read the paper. Brush on the second coat of egg wash, again thinly and evenly. If you apply too much egg wash you are essentially cooking an omelette on the surface of the pastry, which will go soft over time and is therefore especially bad for cold pies.

Rolling Pastry

There are a few simple principles to follow when rolling pastry. Firstly, always work with dough that is well chilled, but not rock hard. This makes the dough easier to handle, avoids the fat splitting while you work and prevents it sticking to the bench. If it's a really hot day, put your thickest chopping board in the refrigerator or freezer until it is well chilled – this will keep the dough as cold as possible while you roll. This is especially useful when rolling and cutting out delicate shapes to decorate pies.

When dusting your work surface, never use too much flour. If the dough is rolled at the right temperature, you shouldn't need much flour at all. The more flour you use, the more you will change the ratio of flour to fat in the dough, which can result in brittleness in the baked pastry. For an even distribution of flour, dust the work surface from a height. Alternatively, try flicking or snapping your wrist to release the flour horizontally in a cloud – this will also make you look like one of those slow-motion chefs from a TV cooking show.

When rolling out dough, always work from the edge closest to you and only roll away from you. Each time you roll the pastry, turn it 90 degrees in the same direction. Don't press downwards during the roll; instead allow the rolling pin to work in a forwards rolling motion. Downwards force will warp the shape and make it harder to achieve what you want. Don't roll all the way over the ends of the dough until you have achieved the shape and size required.

Lining Pie Moulds

The key to lining tins and moulds with pastry is temperature. If you allow the pastry dough to get too warm and soft it will be difficult to manage, easy to stretch and prone to damage. When this occurs, it can cause weak spots in the pastry lining that can potentially crack or burst during cooking, so make sure your dough is always chilled. If you have really warm hands or it is just an unusually hot day, wear latex gloves as this helps to stop the heat transferring from your hands to the dough and also prevents the pastry from sticking to your hands when you press it.

To line a 23cm springform cake tin or similar size round pie tin, first roll 700g of pastry dough on a lightly floured work surface to the size of the largest baking tray that will fit in your refrigerator. Line the tray with parchment paper and lay the pastry on top, then allow it to rest for 30 minutes in the refrigerator or 15 minutes in the freezer (if you have enough space).

Once rested, remove the rolled-out pastry from the refrigerator or freezer and transfer it to your work surface. Roll the pastry out again to a large rectangle roughly 50cm x 80cm and 5mm thick. While the dough is still cold, centre the tin on top of the pastry. Using the tip of a knife, lightly score around the base of the tin and then mark a larger circle that equals the height of the tin plus an extra 2.5cm that will overhang the top edge of the tin. For a 23cm tin, in total you will need a 45cm diameter circle. For an easy way to measure, once you have lightly marked the base, rock the tin onto its side and mark where the top edge of the tin now rests. Repeat around the base circle until you can see the larger outer circle, then cut it out 2.5cm wider all the way round so you have enough pastry for crimping together the lining and the lid (see page 33).

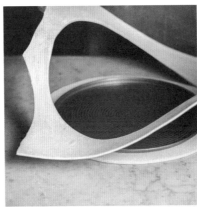

Using the base of the tin as a guide, cut a circle 2.5cm wider from the remaining pastry for the pie lid. Place the lid back on the lined tray and return to the refrigerator until needed. Any pastry trimmings can be cut into smaller sections and chilled with the lid to use for decoration later on.

Lightly grease the base, sides and lip of the tin with a little softened butter (I prefer to use butter over oil as it helps with the caramelisation of the pastry and adds flavour during cooking). Dust off any excess flour from both sides of the pastry. Fold the large disc of pastry in half and then in half again, like a slice of pizza.

Pop the folded pastry inside the tin so the two straight sides line up exactly in one quarter of the tin and then unfold the pastry circle. This is the easiest way to centre the pastry. Work the pastry into the bottom edge of the tin first while being careful not to stretch it. Check there are no air bubbles under the base (you can push these out while still at this stage) and then gently press the pastry against the sides of the tin. Creases in the pastry can open up later when the tin is removed, causing the pie to bulge, so it's important that you don't press firmly initially. Instead, work around the tin fully to begin, making sure the pastry is even and there is 2.5cm of pastry overhanging the top edge for crimping. Finally, press the pastry firmly and evenly against the sides of the tin. I use two or three fingers together to do this. If the pastry is getting soft or your hands are too warm, either wear a pair of latex gloves (as mentioned above) to stop the heat transferring to the pastry or alternatively use an offcut of cold dough lightly dusted with flour.

When the base and sides are firmly pressed against the tin, check the pastry overhanging the top edge that will be used for crimping later. If necessary, trim to an even 2.5cm all round.

Allow the pastry-lined tin to rest for 20 minutes in the refrigerator or 10 minutes in the freezer or until set hard before filling.

To line a 24cm rectangular pie mould or 900g/2lb loaf tin, first roll out 800g of pastry dough on a lightly floured work surface to the size of the largest baking tray that will fit in your refrigerator. Line the tray with parchment paper and lay the pastry on top, then allow it to rest for 30 minutes in the refrigerator or 15 minutes in the freezer (if you have enough space).

Once rested, remove the rolled-out pastry from the refrigerator or freezer and transfer it to your work surface. Roll the pastry out again to a large rectangle at least 50cm x 45cm and 5mm thick. With the slightly longer side of the rolled-out pastry closest to you, cut a 15cm wide strip from the right-hand edge to use for the pie lid. Place the strip back on the lined tray and return to the refrigerator until needed. You will now be left with a 45cm x 35cm rectangle.

While the dough is still cold, centre the tin on top of the pastry. Using the tip of a knife, lightly score around the four corners of the tin for reference. Once you have lightly marked the base, rock the tin onto one long side and mark where the top edge of the tin now rests plus an additional 2.5cm so you have enough pastry for crimping together the lining and the lid (see page 33).

Return the tin to its original position and then rock it over to the opposite long side. Mark this side as before. Repeat this process for the two opposite shorter ends.

Leaving the tin on the pastry to hold it in place, cut along the marked lines, adding an additional 1cm at the end of each line to allow for a small overlap when lining the tin. Now cut a diagonal line from each of the marked base corners to the extended ends of the lines just cut.

Lift the tin off the pastry. You will now have an outline that looks like the tin has been unfolded on the pastry. If the pastry has become too soft to handle, return it to the refrigerator for 10 minutes to chill. Any pastry trimmings can be cut into smaller sections and chilled with the lid to use for decoration later on.

Lightly grease the base, sides and lip of the tin with a little softened butter (again, I prefer to use butter over oil as it helps with the caramelisation of the pastry and adds flavour during cooking). Dust off any excess flour from both sides of the pastry. Fold in the top and bottom flaps onto the base and then fold in the two side flaps on top of the other flaps, so you have a neat package. Drop this pastry package into the tin or mould and carefully unfold all the flaps.

First, make sure that the pastry is sitting right down into the bottom edge on each side. Check that there are no air bubbles under the base (you can push these out while at this stage). Next, firmly press the pastry together at the overlapping corners. If the pastry is getting soft or your hands are too warm, either wear a pair of latex gloves or use an offcut of cold dough lightly dusted with flour.

When the corners are firmly pressed together, start to press the sides against the tin. Always work a little pressure down towards the base of the tin to get the crisp edge at the bottom.

When the sides and corners are firmly pressed against the tin, check the pastry overhanging the top edge that will be used for crimping later. If necessary, trim to an even 2.5cm all round.

Allow the pastry-lined tin to rest for 20 minutes in the refrigerator or for 10 minutes in the freezer or until set hard before filling.

Decoration

With pastry work, you have the opportunity to be creative in both what you put on the outside of the pie as well as the inside. Once your ingredients are wrapped in pastry, you have a blank canvas. In The Pie Room, I encourage the team to throw themselves into this creative process and work on new designs, drawing inspiration from the things around them – from architecture to nature, or anything that catches their eye that might be translated into pastry.

One of the simplest ways to make savoury pastry stand out is by crimping. All my chefs have different styles and I can tell who has made any pie simply by looking at the crimp. I love this bit of personalisation – it's like an artist's signature in the corner of a painting. Two of the easiest crimps are shown here.

The first is my favourite and creates a wave-like crimp that rolls around the edge of a pie. To crimp a single sheet of pastry, for example on the sardine, olive and onion tartlets (page 91), lightly brush 2.5cm of the inside edge of the overhanging pastry with egg wash. Starting at one point or corner, fold over the pastry at a slight angle onto the brushed surface. Now a little wave of pastry has been created, place the tip of your index finger on the outside of that wave and, using the thumb of your other hand, roll another wave onto the brushed pastry. Move your index finger along to the other side of that new wave and repeat the process all the way round. If you continue to turn the pastry in at a slight angle, it will take on that beautiful wave shape.

To crimp together a pastry lid and lining, lightly brush the lip of the lining with egg wash, but don't brush the lid as well – if you do, it won't stick. Line up the lid so it is centred perfectly over the top of the pie. You now need to thin the pastry out, otherwise it will be twice the thickness of any other part of the pie.

Working around the pie lid, firmly squeeze together the two layers of pastry, thinning it out in the process. This will create an excess of overhanging pastry, so, using kitchen scissors, trim it back to 2.5cm to neaten but leaving enough to crimp.

Lightly brush a 2.5cm border around the top of the outside edge with egg wash. Holding your index finger and thumb on one hand about 5cm apart, roll the pastry lip over onto the brushed surface, narrowing the gap just before you pres it down. Moving along another 2.5cm each time, repeat the process all the way round. After you have crimped all the way around, chill the pastry in the fridge for 10 minutes and then brush lightly all over with egg wash.

There are two methods of applying decoration to the surface of a pie. One way is to score the surface of the pastry directly and the other is to add more pastry cut into shapes. For the first option, you must apply egg wash properly. It's important not to slap on lots of egg wash as that results in an uneven finish, and too much egg on the pastry leaves it soft after cooking. Lightly brush a thin, even coat of egg wash all over the surface of the pastry. Pop the pie in the refrigerator for 15 minutes or until the egg wash is almost dry.

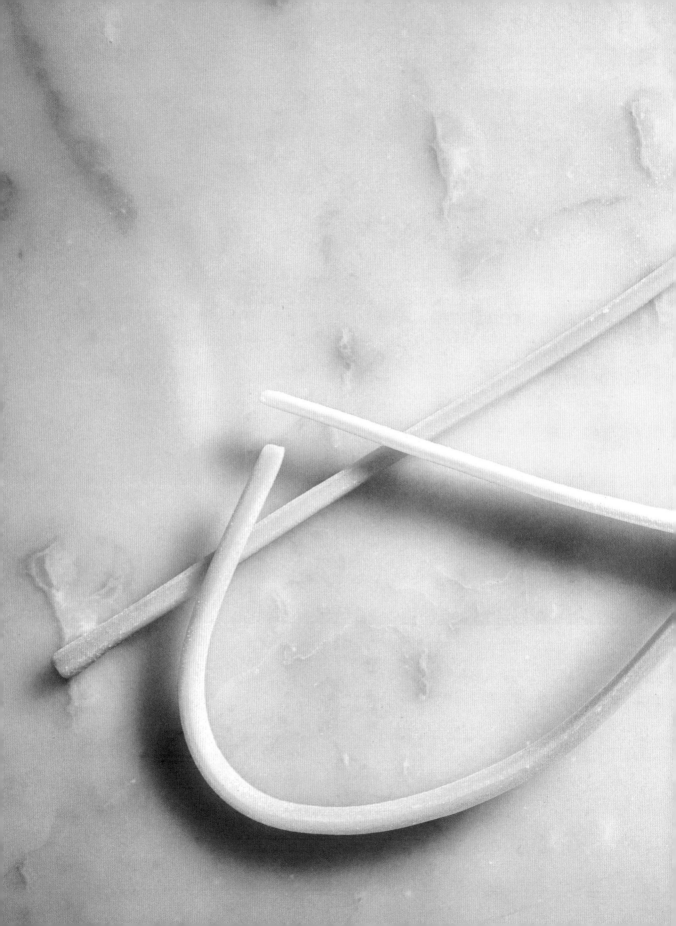

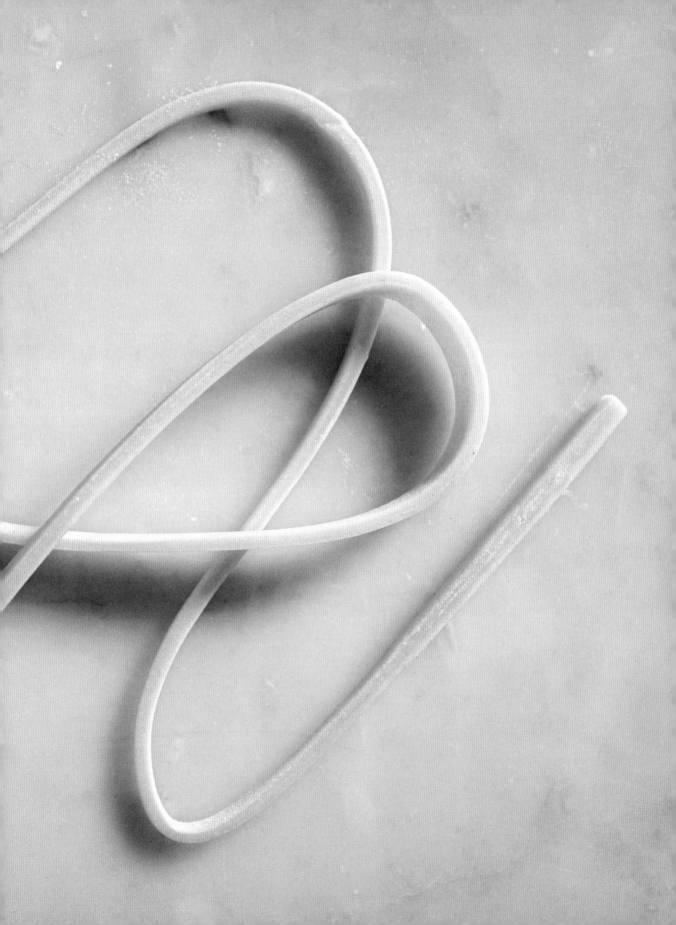

Next, apply a second thin coat of egg wash. Pop the pie back into the refrigerator. After 10 minutes, check the feel of the egg wash; it should be tacky to the touch, not completely dry. If the egg wash dries out too much, it will crack – you will see that in your finished pie – and the pastry may crack or tear during scoring.

You are now ready to score the pastry with decorative lines. Using a small, light knife, score your preferred design into the surface of the pastry. Take care not to score right through the pastry as it will open right up during cooking. Do not egg wash again after scoring as it will simply cover up any design you have made.

To apply shapes to create a design, such as the leaves shown on page 33, first make sure the pastry you are adding is rolled out thinly before cutting, otherwise it will look clunky and lose its shape during cooking. Add the cut-out pastry shapes after the surface of the pie has been egg washed and is just at the tacky stage, but not dry. Do not brush any egg wash onto the shapes you are applying as they won't hold properly. Once in place on the surface of the pie, brush the pastry shapes with egg wash and rest in the refrigerator for 15 minutes. You can lightly score the pastry shapes with a small, light knife to add more detail, taking care not to score right through. The pressure applied when scoring further helps to stick the pastry shapes to the pie.

Plaiting pastry is a way to add an attractive border to a pie and is much simpler than it looks. However, it does require a couple of key things: the right dough at the correct temperature. I prefer to create a plait using shortcrust dough: it has a strong enough structure to be moved around as much as needed and is more forgiving at increased temperatures. As far as possible, the pastry needs to be kept cool as it becomes difficult to turn when warm and soft.

To plait pastry for a decorative border, first roll out the dough into a thin sheet, no more than 5mm thick. The pastry needs to be cold for the next stage to work,

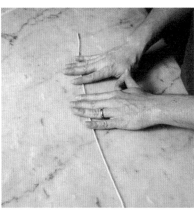

so pop the rolled-out pastry in the refrigerator for 20 minutes. If possible, lay the pastry on a thick chopping board so that chills too. Remove the pastry from the refrigerator and cut it into nine thin strips about 5mm wide. Gently roll each one to take off the sharp edges, leaving you with spaghetti shapes.

Take three of the pastry strips and pinch them together at one end. Repeat with the remaining strips so that you have three bunches each of three strips. Keeping each bunch separate, lay them side by side on your work surface and then pinch all three bunches together at the top. To make the plait, lift the middle bunch over the right bunch, keeping the strips neat. Next, lift what is now the middle bunch over the left bunch. Next, lift the now middle bunch over the right bunch, and then the now middle bunch over the left bunch. Continue working in this way until you reach the end and the plait is complete. Squeeze the three bunches at the end of the plait to seal it and trim away any excess.

To apply the plait to the pie, lightly brush a thin layer of egg wash onto the surface of the pie. Lay the plait on the pie and gently press. Once in place, lightly brush the plait with egg wash, but don't get it too wet as you will lose all that beautiful detail.

Essential Equipment

1. Rolling pin

Invest in a large, heavy wooden rolling pin – it's game-changing. With the exception of a lucky ambidextrous few, we are all right- or left-handed and so will always roll with a slight bias to one side. With a heavy rolling pin this is reduced as the weight of the pin does the majority of the work for you. Having a longer rolling pin also means being able to roll out wider areas of dough more easily without leaving an indent in the middle where you have been forced to roll it out as two halves.

2. Electric stand mixer

Mixing anything over 1kg of dough can be laborious by hand, so an electric stand mixer is extremely useful if you can afford one. Without a mixer, you will transfer the heat from your hands into the dough and so it also helps to keep the pastry cold. I often hear that people's grandmothers didn't use a mixer to make their pastry, but sometimes technology should be embraced if it makes things more suitable to our current lives.

3. Pastry brushes

You can find small pastry brushes in kitchen shops and online. I have quite a few pastry brushes in my collection alongside lots of small, thin paint brushes that I use for really fine detail. Always buy proper brushes with bristles, rather than the rubber or silicone ones you sometimes see – they are far more effective and give a better finish. Make sure all brushes are well cleaned and the bristles are dry before putting them away. I also have a medium-sized brush, which looks more like a decorator's brush, that I use for cleaning up any excess flour on the work surface after rolling out dough.

4. Pastry cutters

I'm always buying new pastry cutters. I must have hundreds. I have leaf-shaped cutters, rabbit-shaped cutters – if you can imagine a shape, I probably have a cutter to match. It's fun to have a variety of different cutters when decorating with pastry, especially when you're working with kids. Adding decorative shapes to a pie is always their favourite part of cooking.

5. Large mixing bowl

It may seem obvious to some, but not everyone has a large mixing bowl in their home kitchen. They are indispensable for efficiently and tidily combining dough mixes. I always keep an extra-large bowl at home with a 4-litre capacity.

6. Springform cake tin

The tin I refer to most often throughout this book is a 23cm round non-stick, springform cake tin. It's the perfect size for making pies serving up to six people. The spring release system means you can pop the pie straight out of the tin without having to turn it out.

7. Loaf tin

Similar in dimensions to the round tin, the loaf tin that I refer to throughout this book is 24cm in length and around 900g/2lb in volume. Again, it is the perfect size for these recipes and, like the round cake tin, always try to buy a non-stick tin.

8. Digital probe thermometer

These are readily available online and also in kitchen shops and are an incredible tool in the kitchen. There are a few recipes in the book where checking the internal temperature of a dish is vital in the method, but you can use it for so much more in your home cooking. I use mine for cooking big joints of meat for a Sunday roast to get perfect rosy beef.

9. Digital weighing scales

While good for weighing out large amounts of ingredients, traditional counter-balanced scales are not so accurate at the other end of the spectrum. Weighing out smaller amounts is where we need accuracy, so it's worth investing in digital weighing scales. Liquids including water and milk can be weighed in grams on scales rather than mls in a measuring jug as there is almost no difference in weight and liquid volume at this end of cooking.

10. Mandoline

The Japanese mandoline has been used in professional kitchens for a long time and is now found more frequently in home kitchens. They are great for slicing potatoes for topping hot pots or for finely cutting vegetables. Always use the guard provided. If you use the mandoline so heavily that it becomes blunt, either have the blade sharpened professionally or buy a new one. A blunt blade is far more dangerous than a sharp one as you have to apply more pressure.

11. Turning knife/paring knife

A small, lightweight knife is perfect for scoring pastry and adding fine detail. I prefer the blade of a turning knife for slightly curved surfaces and tricky corners (as it has a finer tip to the blade) and a paring knife (also known as a vegetable knife) for scoring flat surfaces.

12. Small palette knife

That this is called a knife is a little misleading as it's more of a spatula really but very useful for lifting small pieces of pastry detail and also pressing them onto egg-washed pastry for decoration. It's also incredibly effective for firing bits of pastry at your brother's head.

13. Wide, fine-mesh sieve

A key stage when making any dough, sifting flour should be done using a wide, fine-mesh sieve. Make sure it is completely dry before you use it … and never let your brother borrow it to cook prawns on a barbeque.

14. Lattice roller

These are easily found online and are great for rolling out a quick lattice which is good for bigger items such as a wellington or large tart. The key to using them is to make sure the pastry is pretty cold and to push really firmly onto a completely flat surface. I think the plastic ones are just as good as the metal ones as really you are just cutting through pastry, so save yourself some money! Even when I use a lattice roller, I still like to go back through the cuts that it makes with a paring knife afterwards to make sure they are all going to open properly. There is nothing worse than stretching out a lattice over something and part of it snaps because it doesn't open properly.

15. Scottish scraper

These are perfect for cleaning up flour and dough from your bench but also for slightly wetter doughs like a hot water pastry, where it helps you avoid getting your hands sticky before the dough cools. It is also useful for portioning doughs (as for the stuffed brioche recipe on page 96).

PASTRY DOUGHS

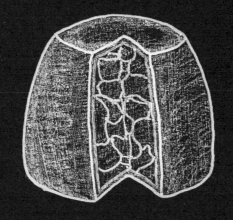

Doughs

Understanding how doughs work, which type you should use for a particular recipe and how to handle that specific dough helps to remove any uncertainty that is often associated with working with pastry. These are some of the tips and tricks that I have picked up over the years – they will give you the confidence to cook at home with pastry.

Pairing your pie filling

The consistency of the pie filling determines the dough you should use. Generally, a wetter filling calls for a pastry with a bit more structure to it, say a shortcrust pastry, whereas a slightly drier filling is able to slip into a more delicate crust, like a puff pastry.

If you are making a sweet pie, look carefully at the ingredients. If it's a fruit filling that has a high sugar content, consider whether you need a sweet pastry or if it would be more balanced with a savoury crust. This is why I prefer to make an apple tart with a savoury pie crust (see page 218). As you work through the recipes in this book, you will see how each filling has been paired with a type of pastry.

Time to rest

Allowing a dough time to rest is so vital in pastry work that, when ignored, it becomes the undoing of many a seasoned chef. Insufficient resting time can lead to cracked, leaking tart cases and undercooked pastry that comes away from the sides of a tin during cooking. When flour is mixed with water it forms strands of gluten, which give the pastry the structure it needs to hold together during baking. Immediately after mixing, the gluten strands in a dough need time to rest and relax, otherwise the pastry will shrink during cooking.

Always allow a dough to rest in the refrigerator before rolling out. Each recipe in this book gives a specific time, but anything less than 30 minutes in the refrigerator or 20 minutes in the freezer will not be long enough to prevent shrinkage.

Keeping it short

Some recipes call for pastry with a more 'mealy' crust. This means a tighter, crumblier crust, which suits a dish like a lemon tart, whereas the pastry top of a chicken pie needs to be light and flaky. The structure of a pastry is, at first, dictated by how well the fat is incorporated into the dough. The longer the fat and flour are mixed then the better the fat coats the flour – this gives the gluten less chance to form long strands and so the pastry will be crumblier. If the fat and flour are mixed for a shorter period of time, this produces a rougher mix – pockets of fat will be left in the dough that bubble up as steam is produced during baking, creating flakes. Puff pastry is an example where both principles are at play. The dough is made with strong flour, which is rich in gluten and forms a strong, structured pastry, but it is then interspersed with layers of fat that create large air pockets to produce the flakes.

The right temperature

Another important principle of pastry work is to keep your dough at the correct temperature. When a dough becomes too warm, the fat melts and splits from the mixture – this is especially disastrous in puff pastry. A warm dough will be too soft to roll out and won't actually move during the rolling process. If it is a hot day and the dough is getting too warm, return the pastry to the refrigerator for a few minutes to chill. An invaluable tip we use in The Pie Room on really hot days is to chill a chopping board in the refrigerator or freezer before rolling out the pastry on it. The cold work surface keeps the pastry pliable ... and helps us keep our cool.

Homemade vs shop-bought

Throughout this book you have the choice of following my recipes for homemade doughs or using shop-bought pastry. This is because I'm a realist. I know how little time people have to cook at home nowadays. You can buy pastry that is made to a great standard, so if you're under pressure to prepare food for a family event it's fine to take this shortcut. There are times when fitting in the half-day process of making a puff pastry simply isn't realistic. Now here's a big reveal … when cooking at home, sometimes I use shop-bought pastry for ease and to save time. I'm not ashamed to say that! Do whatever works for you, but when you do have a moment, take the time to practise the dough recipes on pages 56–73. Making pastry by hand is a great way to understand how pastry works and what each dough feels like, and become comfortable with the different types of crust, plus you have the added satisfaction of creating it all from scratch.

I find pastry work incredibly therapeutic; it's my time to focus on the task in hand and remove myself from the outside world for a little while, but that is only possible when I can afford myself the time.

Recycling pastry dough

Trimmings from each pastry dough recipe in this book can be re-rolled and used once again, although there are a few things to bear in mind when doing so. In the section on rolling techniques (see page 24), you will notice that I recommend not using too much flour when dusting the dough and work surface. This is because any additional flour alters the consistency and structure of the dough, which can make it tough to roll out again and overly fragile during baking. When re-rolling any trimmings, you must allow the dough to rest in the refrigerator again before using. This is because you have put the gluten strands under stress during rolling and so, without a chance to relax, the pastry will shrink back dramatically. If freezing dough trimmings, dust off any excess flour before flattening them into a puck. Wrap the dough well in clingfilm before freezing for up to one month. Classic puff pastry can be re-rolled, but the resulting bake will not be as even and much more like a rough puff pastry.

Flours

Strong flours have a higher protein content than softer flours and can absorb more water. They also develop gluten strands much more easily, making a tougher pastry. Softer and plain flours always work better for flakier crusts.

Due to the boom in real breadmaking within homes over the last ten years, we are lucky to have a huge variety of flours available in supermarkets and food shops. At The Pie Room we use organic flours that are full of nutrients and flavour, which are a joy to work with. For certain doughs we use unbleached, heritage flours milled from grains that were more commonly farmed centuries ago. Wherever you can, like all ingredients in the recipes, I recommend using the best flour that you can afford. Remember that unbleached flours result in a much darker crust, as you will see with the pork pie (see page 86), as well as the most incredible flavour – and that wins for me every time.

The most important thing to remember when using any flour is to sift. Wherever a pack of flour has been stored, be it in the cupboard at home or on a supermarket shelf, it could have absorbed moisture and formed lumps inside. It takes just a minute to sift flour through a sieve to remove any lumps. If you don't sift and then find a lump of raw flour in a crust at the end of cooking, there's little you can do about it. Always sift.

Fats

The most commonly used fat throughout this book is butter. It dominates the dough chapter and features heavily in many of the savoury recipes. In the ingredients list for each recipe, you may notice that I never state which type of butter to use in the pastry recipes. That is because I use salted butter as standard for everything that I bake. Because it's so tasty, salted butter is the butter that I keep in my refrigerator at home for all my cooking. The slight savoury note salted butter adds to everything will only be a bonus; even sweet dishes will benefit from the balance gifted by a little salt. As with flour, use the best butter you can afford for these recipes. Anything that is left over will be amazing spread on hot toast in the morning.

Both suet and lard are widely available in supermarkets. If not, suet can be easily ordered online. In The Pie Room, the type of lard we use is called leaf lard, which is fat taken from around the pig's kidneys. Leaf lard is very pure and not overly strong-flavoured – it makes a beautifully clean-tasting pastry. I'm lucky to get mine from a friend who makes charcuterie, but you could ask your local butcher if they can source it for you or look online if you are keen to try it for yourself.

Shortcrust Pastry

The first recorded recipe for shortcrust pastry goes back to the eighteenth century so it's been with us for a long time, keeping pies happily wrapped up and rightly so. It's a cracking dough. It is superb for savoury pies and tart cases that need more robust structural integrity than puff pastry provides. If the flour and butter are blended completely in a food processor until they resemble a crumble mix before the wet ingredients are added, the pastry will have a more mealy texture, which is often better for tart cases. Making the pastry by hand results in a flakier pastry with a fine crumb. The level of flakiness can be managed by how thoroughly the flour is mixed with the butter. If the butter is left in slightly larger, more visible nuggets within the pastry dough, you will get a flakier result because the butter melts in pockets during cooking, allowing flakes to form as the water in the dough creates steam and puffs the pockets. Be very careful not to overwork this dough, as mentioned in the recipe, as otherwise you will create gluten strands that are too long, and it will become tough and chewy.

This is probably my favourite dough, and it's the most versatile I can think of with applications from the flakiest apple pie lid to the fine detail of a pastry braid, and with proper seasoning as in the recipe below, it is absolutely delicious to eat.

MAKES ABOUT 900G (OR ENOUGH TO LINE TWO 25CM ROUND TART TINS)

2 eggs, beaten
60ml ice-cold water
500g plain flour
10g fine table salt
250g butter, chilled and diced
    into 2cm cubes

Combine the beaten egg with the ice-cold water and keep it in the refrigerator until needed. It is important to keep this egg mixture chilled as it will shock the butter back to coldness and stop it from splitting.

If making the pastry by hand, sift the flour and salt into a mixing bowl. Add the butter cubes and, using a round-bladed knife, cut the butter into the flour until the pieces are as small as possible. Working quickly, pass a handful of flour and butter across your fingertips, gently rubbing them together as you allow it to fall back into the bowl, until the mixture looks like breadcrumbs.

If making the pastry using a mixer, sift the flour into the bowl and add the salt and butter. Using a paddle attachment, work at a medium speed to incorporate the butter into the flour.

Whether working by hand or using a mixer, continue working the butter into the flour until the butter is almost incorporated but small nuggets are still visible (for a flaky pastry) or fully incorporated to a fine granular mix (for a mealy, more even pastry).

Make a well in the middle of the flour and pour in the chilled egg mixture. Continue to work by hand with the round-bladed knife or with the mixer on a medium speed until the dough just starts to come together. The dough should still be fairly rough – it is important not to overwork the dough at this point otherwise gluten in the flour will form strong bonds and the pastry will develop an undesirable elasticity.

Tip the dough out onto a lightly floured surface and gently knead it a few times to finish. Be careful not to overwork or handle it too much. Flatten the dough into a rectangle, wrap it tightly in clingfilm and chill in the refrigerator for at least 30 minutes, but preferably 1 hour, before using.

This shortcrust pastry dough can be kept for up to three days in the refrigerator or up to one month in the freezer. If freezing, weigh out the dough into the quantities needed for individual recipes – it will take less time to thaw and you won't be potentially wasting any dough. To use the dough from the freezer, allow it to come back to refrigerator temperature overnight.

Sweet Shortcrust Pastry

While some doughs for dessert tarts and pies do not require any sweetness, others do. This is all down to the sugar content of the filling itself. If the filling is tart, it may benefit from a little additional sweetness. The recipes in this book specify whether to use a sweet or savoury shortcrust pastry. Over the years I have collected so many sweet pastry recipes. The instructions below combine various elements from these different recipes, blending what I feel worked well in each of them to make the ultimate sweet pastry. The structure of this pastry is strong and so lends itself well to blind baking and slices cleanly when serving. It also has just the right balance of savoury and sweet notes. It is important to not overwork the dough and allow it plenty of resting time in order to stop it shrinking during the baking process.

MAKES ABOUT 1KG (OR ENOUGH TO LINE TWO 25CM ROUND TART TINS)

250g butter, chilled and diced
    into 2cm cubes
180g caster sugar
½ teaspoon vanilla extract
500g plain flour
a large pinch of fine table salt
2 eggs, beaten

If making the pastry by hand, place the butter, sugar and vanilla extract in a bowl. Using a wooden spoon, cream together the ingredients until the mixture is light, fluffy and pale in colour. Scrape down the sides of the bowl.

If making the pastry using a mixer, place the butter, sugar and vanilla extract in the bowl. Using a paddle attachment, work at a medium speed to cream together the ingredients. After mixing for 1 minute, stop the mixer and scrape down the sides of the bowl and the paddle. Continue working at a medium speed for about 4–5 minutes or until the mixture is light, fluffy and pale in colour. Take the bowl off the stand. Scrape any mixture from the paddle into the bowl.

Sift the flour and salt into the bowl with the butter mixture and, using a large metal spoon, gently fold into the mixture until the flour is incorporated. If using a mixer, replace the bowl on the stand and continue to mix at a medium speed until a crumbly consistency.

While beating, gradually add one-quarter of the beaten egg and mix until fully incorporated. Gradually add the remaining egg, one-quarter at a time, until all the beaten egg is fully combined and the dough is smooth.

Flatten the dough into a rectangle, wrap it tightly in clingfilm and rest in the refrigerator for at least 30 minutes, but preferably 1 hour, before using.

This sweet shortcrust pastry dough can be kept for up to three days in the refrigerator or up to one month in the freezer. If freezing, weigh out the dough into the quantities needed for individual recipes – it will take less time to thaw and you won't be potentially wasting any dough. To use the dough from the freezer, allow it to come back to refrigerator temperature overnight.

Hot Water Crust Pastry

Traditionally used to encase cold pork pies, hot water crust pastry is one of the oldest British pie dough recipes. With early origins showing ingredients as just flour and hot water, it was likely in the Medieval times that it developed into what we now more closely know: flour, hot water and lard. It would have been used to make huge pies for banquets, encasing goose, venison and whole swans. Over time this pastry technique has changed little; it is still worked with while hot as it firms up as it cools. In The Pie Room, however, we have worked hard at adapting the traditional recipe to form a slightly lighter, crispier crust, that is fresh with the flavour of herbs and that can be worked with at a cooler room temperature and even used again after refrigeration.

MAKES 1KG

Combine the water, lard, rosemary and salt in a medium saucepan. Bring to the boil, then reduce to a simmer and wait for the lard to melt fully, then turn off the heat and allow to infuse.

Sift the flour into a bowl. Using either a round-bladed knife or the paddle attachment of a mixer, start to work on a medium speed. Add the egg and mix until thoroughly dispersed through the flour – this will take 2–3 minutes.

Remove the rosemary from the pan with a fork and then bring the water and fat mix to a boil. Slowly pour onto the flour and egg mix, scraping the bowl and paddle halfway through to prevent any lumps from forming. Mix for 2–3 minutes until well combined.

Allow the dough to cool on a tray between parchment paper until the heat has dissipated and then chill for 10 minutes in the refrigerator before using.

This hot water crust pastry dough can be kept for up to three days in the refrigerator or one month in the freezer. If freezing, weigh out the dough into the quantities needed for individual recipes – it will take less time to thaw and you won't be potentially wasting any dough. To use the dough from the freezer, allow it to come back to refrigerator temperature overnight.

200ml water
160g lard
2 rosemary sprigs
10g salt
500g plain flour
2 eggs, beaten

Classic Puff Pastry

I always assumed puff pastry was invented in France. It is so dominant throughout French food culture, evident in the windows of every pâtisserie, that this is an easy assumption to make. However, Spanish recipes for puff pastry precede the French with the first documented appearance right at the beginning of the seventeenth century, while the first French recipe appears mid-century.

A classic butter puff pastry is a laminated dough that rises due to the power of steam. When making the dough, many thin, alternating layers of fat and dough are created so that, when cooked at a high enough heat, the fat melts to leave a pocket of air in the dough. The moisture in the dough and fat then boils to create steam, which causes these pockets to expand. Before you cook puff pastry, it is important to make sure the oven is at the correct temperature so that this transformative process occurs quickly, allowing the structure to form and be locked in.

This recipe creates a puff pastry that rises evenly and is neater than rough puff, so it is better suited to dishes like vol au vents where a little refinement is needed. Honestly, it is a myth that puff pastry is difficult to make. All that is required for success is planning, patience, and following the instructions closely. This recipe creates a large batch of dough – if you're going to spend an afternoon making puff pastry, you may as well make plenty – so divide it into smaller amounts based on the recipes you plan to make before wrapping and freezing for later use.

MAKES 1.5KG

First prepare the dough. If making the pastry by hand, sift the flour into a large bowl and add the salt, butter and water. Using your fingers, gently mix to an even dough. Transfer the dough to a lightly floured surface and knead it for 5 minutes or until smooth.

If making the pastry using a mixer, sift the flour into the mixer bowl and add the salt, butter and water. Using a dough hook, work at a medium speed for a few minutes to incorporate the butter into the flour until it forms a smooth dough.

Flatten the dough into a neat rectangle, wrap it tightly in clingfilm and rest in the refrigerator for 45 minutes.

For the dough
350g strong flour
200g plain flour
15g table salt
115g butter, softened and diced
250ml ice-cold water

For the lock-in butter
500g chilled butter, diced
50g strong flour

...continued on page 64

Meanwhile, prepare the lock-in butter. Thoroughly clean and dry the bowl and line a baking tray with parchment paper. Place the butter and flour in the bowl and either work the flour into the butter using a wooden spoon for 5–10 minutes, or use the mixer working at a low speed for 2 minutes or until everything is well incorporated. Scrape the butter mixture onto the lined tray and, using floured hands, shape it into a square about 1cm thick. Place the butter mixture in the refrigerator until just chilled but not completely hard. (It is important that the chilled dough and lock-in butter are similarly firm, otherwise they will not roll together evenly and this may cause rips and holes in the dough.)

On a lightly floured surface, roll out the dough into a large square that is twice the size of the lock-in butter. Place the butter in the centre of the dough but at an angle so that the corners point towards the edges of the dough. Making sure you do not trap any air, fold the corners of the dough over the butter, bringing them into the middle like an envelope. Lightly pinch together all the joins to seal and completely encase the butter.

Roll out the dough and butter into a rectangle roughly three times as long as it is wide, using the sides of your hands to make sure the edges are neat and square. Dust any excess flour from the surface of the dough. With the shortest side closest to you, visually divide the dough horizontally into thirds and very lightly dampen the centre third with a little water, then fold the bottom one third of the dough over the centre third. Repeat by folding the remaining top third over the double layer of dough, then tightly wrap the dough in clingfilm. Lightly press your finger into the bottom right-hand corner of the dough to make an indentation which signifies the first turn and how the dough was positioned on the board before you put it into the refrigerator.

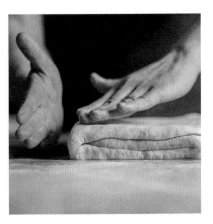

Chill the dough in the refrigerator for 30 minutes. (Chilling the pastry between each roll out and fold allow the butter to harden so that clean, even layers of dough and butter are built up.)

Unwrap the dough and place it on a lightly floured surface with the indent in the same position as before at the bottom right-hand corner. Next, turn the dough 90 degrees clockwise. Roll out the dough into an 18cm by 25cm rectangle and repeat the folding process. Make sure all corners and sides are straight. Wrap the dough in clingfilm again and this time make two indents on the dough in the bottom right corner. Chill in the refrigerator for a further 30 minutes.

Repeat the turning and folding processes two more times, each time chilling the dough for 30 minutes and marking with indents in the bottom right-hand corner to make sure the dough is turned in the correct direction. After the final turn, chill the dough in the refrigerator for 45 minutes and then it is ready to use.

This classic puff pastry dough can be kept for up to three days in the refrigerator or one month in the freezer. If freezing, weigh out the dough into the quantities needed for individual recipes – it will take less time to thaw and you won't be potentially wasting any dough. To use the dough from the freezer, allow it to come back to refrigerator temperature overnight.

Rough Puff Pastry

This is a quicker, simpler dough to make than the classic puff pastry. However, it does result in a more rustic and uneven rise, but that is not always such a terrible thing. I actually prefer rough puff pastry for certain pies specifically because it lends that homely look. Rough puff will rise only to about 70 percent of the height of a classic puff, so misses some of the drama, but it is a good entry-level dough to make first in the lead-up to building a properly laminated classic puff pastry. This recipe creates a large batch of pastry, so divide it into smaller amounts based on the recipes you plan to make before wrapping and freezing for later use.

MAKES 1.25KG

500g plain flour
1 teaspoon fine table salt
500g butter, chilled and diced
250ml ice-cold water

If making the pastry by hand, sift the flour into a large bowl and add the salt and butter. Using your fingers, gently mix to a rough dough.

If making the pastry using a mixer, sift the flour into the bowl and add the salt and butter. Using a paddle attachment, work at a medium speed for 2–3 minutes until the butter has formed small nuggets and the mixture becomes grainy.

Add the ice-cold water all at once to the flour and butter and continue at a medium speed just to bring the dough together. The dough should not be well mixed; you want the dough to be straggly and rough, with the fats still visible, so don't work it for too long.

Tip the mixture out onto a lightly floured surface and carefully knead the dough until all the flour is incorporated. Flatten the dough slightly, wrap it tightly in clingfilm and chill in the refrigerator for 30 minutes.

On a lightly floured surface, roll out the dough to a rectangle measuring 50cm by 30cm, using the sides of your hands to make sure the edges are neat and square. Dust any excess flour from the surface of the dough. With the shortest side closest to you, visually divide the dough horizontally into thirds and very lightly dampen the centre third with a little water, then fold the bottom one third of the dough over the centre third. Repeat by folding the remaining top third over the double layer of dough.

Turn the dough 90 degrees clockwise and repeat the rolling and folding process. This makes up the first two turns. Tightly wrap the dough in clingfilm. Lightly press your finger into the bottom right-hand corner of the dough to make an indentation which signifies how the dough was positioned on the board before you put it into the refrigerator. Chill the dough in the refrigerator for 30 minutes.

Unwrap the dough and place it on your work surface with the indent in the same position as before at the bottom right-hand corner. Next, turn the dough 90 degrees clockwise and repeat the rolling and folding processes two more times for the final two turns. Chill in the refrigerator for at least 40 minutes before it is ready to use.

This rough puff pastry dough can be kept for up to three days in the refrigerator or one month in the freezer. If freezing, weigh out the dough into the quantities needed for individual recipes – it will take less time to thaw and you won't be potentially wasting any dough. To use the dough from the freezer, allow it to come back to refrigerator temperature overnight.

Suet Pastry

Another ancient British pastry recipe, this dough includes an interesting ingredient not commonly used much nowadays. Suet is the very hard fat from around the main organs of generally either beef or lamb. As it cannot be rubbed into flour in the conventional way, instead suet is shredded and just incorporated into the dough to melt later during the cooking process. Of course, this is a good thing for flaky pie tops as those melting fats leave air pockets for flakes to form in a bake, and when the pastry is steamed (as in a steamed steak and kidney pudding), it keeps the pastry moist during the cooking process. While best used straight away due to the self-raising content of the flour, which adds lightness to the finished pastry, suet pastry can be refrigerated or frozen to be baked at a later date, but it will not rise quite as much. My old boss Marcus Verberne first taught me how to make this at Roast restaurant. I remember watching him grate frozen butter on a cheese grater for the first time and thinking 'What is this guy doing?!' Now I know why – it is a great recipe that we've changed very little since.

MAKES 1KG

150g butter, frozen
550g self-raising flour
210g shredded suet, very cold
10g table salt
half a bunch of thyme, leaves
    picked
250ml ice-cold water

Grate the frozen butter into a metal bowl and then pop it straight back into the freezer until needed.

Sift the flour into the bowl of an electric mixer. Using a paddle attachment, working at a slow speed, and the grated butter, suet, salt and thyme. Mix for 2 minutes. Slowly add the ice-cold water until the dough just comes together. Remove the dough from the mixer and finish by hand until the flour is incorporated but the fats are still visible.

Flatten the dough slightly and then wrap it tightly in clingfilm. Put the dough in the refrigerator to chill for 30 minutes before using.

This suet pastry dough can be kept for up to three days in the refrigerator or one month in the freezer. However it is likely to rise a bit less due to the activation of the self-raising flour in the early stages. To defrost, remove from the freezer and transfer to the fridge the day before you want to use it.

Choux Pastry

Choux is more than just profiteroles and éclairs. In fairness, I have a weak spot for both of those delicacies, but choux pastry is incredible when used in savoury dishes, too. Its origins can be traced back as far as the sixteenth century with the term 'choux' appearing in the eighteenth century, when French pastry chef Avice used it to create his famous buns which resembled cabbages or 'choux' in French. As is often claimed in modern French recipes, Antonin Carême had a hand in adapting choux pastry into the version that we know today, using it to create huge centrepieces at Royal banquets.

It is important to use strong flour for choux pastry as its higher protein content means it can absorb more liquid; the greater amount of egg means the pastry has a lighter finish at the end. The protein in strong flour also means it develops more gluten strands, giving the pastry the elasticity needed for expansion during cooking but without bursting.

MAKES 500G

Pour the milk and water into a medium, non-stick saucepan and add the butter and salt. Bring to the boil over a high heat and then as soon as all the butter has melted, reduce the heat to medium. Add the sifted flour to the pan all at once, then cook for 3 minutes or until smooth, stirring continuously with a wooden spoon; reduce the heat if you feel the choux paste is catching on the base of the pan.

Transfer the choux paste to a mixer. Using the paddle attachment, beat on a medium speed for 30 seconds to take some of the heat out of the paste. While beating at a medium speed, gradually add one-quarter of the beaten egg and mix until the egg is fully incorporated. Continue adding the egg gradually, one-quarter at a time, until all the beaten egg is fully combined. Continue to beat the choux paste until it is perfectly smooth and has a sheen to it. When pinched lightly, the paste should retain its shape.

This choux pastry dough can be kept for up to three days in the refrigerator or one month in the freezer. If freezing, I pipe the dough onto a tray in the required shapes first and then freeze them, before transferring to a storage container. Pre-piped choux pastry can be cooked straight from frozen and achieves very similar results to when cooked from fresh. However, you will need to increase the cooking time to account for defrosting the dough.

120ml whole milk
110ml water
60g butter, diced
a large pinch of fine table salt
65g strong flour, sifted
2 eggs, beaten

Brioche Dough

With a structure that sits somewhere between bread and cake, brioche dough is heavily enriched with butter and works equally well for both sweet and savoury dishes. Largely believed to be French in origin, brioche recipes have swung from a lighter version to a richer one and back again many times throughout its history for economic reasons: the cost of the butter added. This is an overnight recipe, so you can make it in the evening to use for brunch or lunch the following day. The long fermentation process allows a beautiful structure to form so that you end up with a tufty, bread-like feel to the dough.

———————————— MAKES ABOUT 1KG ————————————

450g strong white flour, plus
   extra for dusting
8g instant dried yeast
15g caster sugar
10g table salt
3 eggs, beaten
90ml whole milk
275g butter, diced

Sift the flour into a bowl, then add the dried yeast, sugar and salt. Using either a round-bladed knife or the dough hook attachment of a mixer, start to combine the ingredients on a slow speed so that the dough doesn't get too warm.

Add the eggs and milk and continue to mix on a slow speed for 5 minutes until the dough is elastic and glossy. Gradually add the butter one-quarter at a time, scraping down the sides of the bowl from time to time, until it is fully incorporated into the dough.

Continue to mix on a slow speed until the dough comes away from the side of the bowl. It's important not to overwork the dough or to work it too fast as any addition of heat will cause the butter to split from the mixture. The dough will be very soft at this point.

If kneading by hand, take a lump of the dough and pull it up vertically, then push it back down and away from you. Continue until the dough becomes smooth and elastic, and forms a ball. To add the butter by hand, turn the dough on to a work surface, bury the butter a tablespoon at a time in the centre of the dough then knead until it becomes a smooth, silky mass. Continue adding butter this way until it has all been added.

Take a bowl larger than the dough and lightly dust it with flour, shake out any excess and place the dough in the bowl. Cover with clingfilm or a dish towel and put it in the refrigerator. Leave the dough to prove for at least 7 hours or overnight. The dough will firm up and be easier to shape.

This brioche dough can be kept for up to three days in the refrigerator or two weeks in the freezer. To defrost, remove from the freezer and transfer to the fridge the day before you want to use it.

Filo Pastry

Filo pastry can be made by hand at home, but should it be?... I've made filo pastry and it takes a lot of time and patience to create a batch large enough for any recipe. The reality here is that, genuinely, I think you should always use shop-bought filo. Unlike other pastries that I have given recipes for, I don't see a big enough difference in handmade and shop-bought filo that justifies the time needed to make it. I even use pre-made filo pastry at the Holborn Dining Room, whenever we need it – there, I've said it. This book is all about making pastry accessible to the home cook, so I want common sense to prevail. For goodness sake, unless you have all the time in the world, buy pre-made filo pastry from a supermarket.

STARTERS & SNACKS

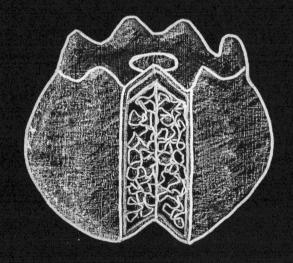

The Ultimate Sausage Roll

In an attempt to find the perfect example, we have tested different flavours and textures for the filling of our sausage rolls at The Pie Room. It always comes back to one thing: simplicity. The filling should be tasty but not overcrowded with too many flavours and textures. The addition of a little chopped bacon and a few thyme leaves to Cumberland sausagemeat are the only changes we make, but the devil is in the detail. For me, the key to the Ultimate Sausage Roll actually lies in the ratio of meat to pastry. When the meat takes longer to cook, the crisper the pastry will be.

―――――――――――――――――― SERVES 4 ――――――――――――――――――

400g rough puff pastry (see
   page 66, or shop-bought
   puff pastry)
2 egg yolks beaten with
   2 teaspoons water,
   for brushing
pinch of black sesame seeds
pinch of white sesame seeds
Plum and Star Anise Chutney,
   to serve (see page 248)

For the filling
700g Cumberland sausages,
   skins removed
150g streaky bacon,
   finely chopped
25g thyme, leaves picked
1/3 teaspoon table salt
large pinch of freshly ground
   black pepper

Equipment
large plastic piping bag
   (optional)

Line a large baking tray with parchment paper. On a lightly floured surface, roll the pastry out to 5mm thick in a 40cm x 25cm rectangle. Slide the rolled-out pastry onto the lined tray and chill in the refrigerator for 30 minutes.

Meanwhile, put the sausagemeat, bacon, thyme, salt and pepper into a bowl and mix well with your hands. Fill a large plastic piping bag with the sausagemeat filling. If you don't have a piping bag, shape the filling into a 6cm wide sausage and wrap tightly in clingfilm, firmly twisting the ends. Chill the filling in the refrigerator for 20 minutes.

Remove the rolled-out pastry from the refrigerator and dust off any excess flour from the surface. Leave the pastry on the parchment paper.

Using kitchen scissors, snip the tip of the piping bag to make a 5cm wide opening. Working from one end of the pastry rectangle, slowly pipe the sausagemeat filling down the length of the pastry 6cm inside one edge. Alternatively, remove the clingfilm from the sausagemeat, unwrapping it over the pastry rectangle, and place the filling 6cm inside one edge of the pastry.

Lightly brush the larger exposed area of pastry all over with egg wash, leaving the narrow 6cm border clear. Fold the egg-washed pastry over the filling to meet the narrow border, align the pastry edges and press firmly together.

Lightly dust the tines of a fork with flour and tap off any excess. Working down the length of the seam, firmly press the ends of the fork into the pastry to leave an impression of the tines. Whenever necessary, dust the fork with more flour to stop it sticking to the pastry.

...continued on page 78

Lightly brush the sausage roll all over with egg wash and return to the refrigerator for 10 minutes to allow the egg wash to dry. Brush a second layer of egg wash over the sausage roll and then, using a sharp knife, lightly score the top of the pastry with diagonal lines all the way down its length. (This gives the pastry a little stretching room and stops it from tearing open at the seam.) Return the sausage roll to the refrigerator to chill for a further 10 minutes.

Preheat the oven to 190°C fan/210°C/gas mark 6½.

Trim a little off the fluted seam of the pastry to neaten it into a straight edge, then brush a final layer of egg wash all over the sausage roll. Sprinkle the black and white sesame seeds along the top of the roll. Pop the tray into the preheated oven and bake the sausage roll for 25 minutes. Check the internal temperature of the filling with a digital probe thermometer – you are looking for 75°C or above. If necessary, return the sausage roll to the oven and check the temperature again every 5 minutes until it reaches 75°C. Alternatively, insert a metal skewer into the centre of the sausage roll and then press it against your hand – it should be very hot to the touch.

Remove the tray from the oven and transfer the sausage roll to a wire cooling rack. Leave to cool for 10 minutes before cutting the sausage roll with a serrated knife into eight equal slices. Serve warm with spoonfuls of chutney.

Gala Pie

The gala pie is an evolution of the classic pork pie. The addition of boiled egg to the centre of the filling instantly catapults this pie to British picnic dish status. When I first started working on this recipe, I always wondered why you never see a gala pie with a gently cooked, soft egg, rather than the usual greying or pale yellow, chalky yolk that is so unappealing. That became my first focus, working out the correct egg to meat and pastry ratio so that the egg yolk remains just soft while the meat and pastry are well cooked. The results are a beautiful slice!

———————————————————— SERVES 6-8 ————————————————————

Bring a pan of water to the boil and fill a large bowl with iced water and keep it close by. Carefully lower the eggs into the boiling water with a spoon, making sure you don't crack them on the base of the pan, and boil for 6 minutes. Remove the eggs from the pan using a slotted spoon and transfer to the bowl of iced water. Leave the eggs to cool for 10 minutes and then once cool enough to handle, peel the shells from the eggs and set aside on paper towels in the refrigerator.

Grease the loaf tin with the butter. Lay a strip of parchment paper along the base of the tin allowing the ends to overhang the sides. (This will help to remove the pie from the tin once cooked.)

On a lightly floured surface, roll out one-third of the dough to a 5mm thick strip long enough to cover the top of the tin. Lay this strip on a tray and place in the refrigerator until needed. Roll out the remaining dough into a large rectangle 5mm thick. Use the remaining dough to line the prepared tin, making sure there is a 2cm excess of pastry overhanging each edge. Put the pastry-lined tin into the freezer for 15 minutes or until the dough has set hard.

Place the pork mince, sausagemeat, bacon, sage and salt in a bowl and mix together with your hands until well combined. Weigh the filling mixture and divide it into two equal halves. Put half the filling mixture into the pastry-lined loaf tin, packing it down and forming a small trench along the centre of the filling for the eggs to nestle in.

Using a sharp knife, take a thin slice off the top and bottom of each boiled egg (being careful not to slice into the yolk). Line up the eggs along the trench in the pie filling. Cover the eggs with the remaining pie filling, gently packing the meat down.

...continued on page 81

600g shortcrust pastry
  (see page 56)
10g butter, for greasing
1 egg yolk beaten with
  1 teaspoon water,
  for brushing
Piccalilli, to serve
  (see page 249)

For the pie filling
6–8 medium organic eggs,
  at room temperature
850g coarsely ground
  pork mince
200g Cumberland sausages,
  skins removed
200g streaky bacon, cut into
  2cm strips
50g sage, leaves picked and
  finely chopped
1½ teaspoons fine table salt

For the jelly
6 bronze gelatine leaves
100ml dry cider
250ml hot pork or beef stock
3 sage leaves
½ teaspoon fine table salt

Equipment
900g (2lb) loaf tin and digital
  probe thermometer

Lightly brush the overhanging edges of the pastry case with the egg wash. Take the strip of pastry out of the refrigerator and lay it across the top of the pie to form the lid. Firmly crimp together the overhanging pastry edges and the pie lid (see page 32 for the crimping technique). Brush the top of the pie with more of the egg wash and chill in the refrigerator for 15 minutes. Score the lid of the pie with diagonal lines (being careful not to cut right through the pastry), then using a small 2cm cutter (or the lid of a pen), make 4 or 5 holes in the pie lid, spacing them evenly along the length of the lid. (This will allow steam to escape from the pie during cooking.) You can add little collars to the steam holes by cutting out slightly larger circles of pastry and punching the same-sized holes out of those, lightly brushing them with egg wash and attaching.

Roll strips of tin foil around a pen to create 5cm long chimneys, and poke them into the steam holes (expanding them slightly when they are inside until they touch the edges) to help any fat escaping during cooking travel up them, rather than across the surface of the pie.

Preheat the oven to 180°C fan/200°C/gas mark 6.

Bake in the preheated oven for 1 hour or until the central temperature of the pie reads 50°C on a digital probe thermometer. Once the pie is at temperature, remove from the oven and allow to rest for 30 minutes.

To make the jelly, put the gelatine leaves in a bowl with enough cold water to cover and add a few ice cubes. Leave to soften.

Bring the cider to the boil in a small saucepan and reduce by two-thirds. Add the stock, sage and salt. Squeeze the gelatine to remove any excess water and then whisk into the hot stock. Pass the mixture through a sieve and then, preferably using a funnel, carefully pour the jelly mixture through the steam holes of the pie until it is full up. Refrigerate for at least 1 hour before serving.

Using the overhanging ends of the parchment paper, lift the pie out of the tin and place on a board. Using a serrated knife, cut the pie into thick slices and serve with spoonfuls of piccalilli.

Prawn Thermidor Vol-au-Vents

Thermidor is one of my all-time favourite dishes, but it is usually served as tender
lobster meat in an inedible shell. I've always believed everything on a plate should
be edible, hence the pastry tart case, which actually adds a lightness to the dish.
At the Holborn Dining Room, we serve a version of this Thermidor tart with lobster,
which you can substitute for the prawns if you are feeling flash.

_____ MAKES 5 _____

200g raw tiger prawns, peeled
20g butter
1 quantity of Hollandaise Sauce
  (see page 258)
25g tarragon leaves, picked
  and chopped, plus extra
  to garnish
100g Gruyère cheese,
  finely grated
1 teaspoon English mustard
5 vol-au-vent cases
  (see page 95)

Preheat the oven to 190°C fan/210°C/gas mark 6½.

Slice each prawn in half horizontally. Heat the butter in a frying pan over a
medium heat. When the butter starts to bubble, add the prawns to the pan
and toss in the butter for 1 minute until just pink. Remove the prawns from
the pan, drain and transfer to paper towels to remove any excess moisture.

Pour the hollandaise sauce into a mixing bowl. Add the tarragon leaves,
Gruyère and mustard to the bowl and fold through the sauce. Lastly, add
the just-cooked prawns.

Place the baked vol-au-vent cases on a baking tray. Spoon the Thermidor
mixture into the vol-au-vent cases, dividing the prawns equally. Fill the
cases so that the Thermidor mixture is just above the rim of the pastry. If
any bubbles over the top during baking, it only makes the dish look even
tastier at the table.

Place the tray in the preheated oven and bake for 10 minutes. Check the
temperature of the Thermidor mixture in the middle with a digital probe
thermometer, it should read 65°C or above. If not, pop the tray back in the
oven for a further few minutes before serving, topped with a few extra
tarragon leaves.

Hot Pork Pie

For centuries, pork pies have firmly held a place in British food culture as a way to use up cuts of pork less desirable than, say, fillet or loin, but truly delicious when handled with care. The most common style of pork pie found in the UK is the cold, jellied picnic pie, however my preferred way to serve a pork pie is piping hot, just out of the oven. The pastry is crispier, the fats are still unctuous, juicy and melting, and the herbs are fragrant.

The first time I ate a hot pork pie was at a pub in the West Country: I remember so clearly wondering why we had never served a hot version in the Holborn Dining Room. As soon as I went back to work, I immediately set about rectifying that. In this recipe, a traditional pork pie dolly (a smooth wooden tool) is used to shape the dough. You can find a dolly easily online, but you could also use a jam jar or a well-buttered metal ring of the same diameter. Roll the pastry into a circle, use it to line the ring, fill and press on a lid, then carefully remove the pie from the ring. Try using a dolly though – you will feel like a character from a Dickens novel (dressing up as one is not necessary, though fully applauded).

SERVES 4

800g hot water crust pastry
  (see page 59)
plain flour, for dusting
2 egg yolks beaten with
  1 teaspoon water,
  for brushing

For the filling
500g pork shoulder, half
  minced and half roughly
  chopped
120g smoked streaky bacon,
  roughly chopped
100g lardo, cut into 1cm dice
1 teaspoon fennel seeds
1 teaspoon yellow
  mustard seeds
1½ teaspoons fine table salt
30g sage, leaves picked and
  finely chopped
a few good twists of freshly
  ground black pepper

Line a baking tray with parchment paper.

Weigh out the pastry dough into four balls weighing 150g and four smaller balls weighing 40g. On a lightly floured surface, flatten the 40g dough balls and roll out to 5mm thick circles. Lay the pastry circles on the lined baking tray and chill in the refrigerator until needed.

Combine all the ingredients for the filling in a mixing bowl. Using your hands, work everything well for a few minutes until the mixture holds together. Split the mixture evenly into four balls and set aside.

Take one of the 150g dough balls and gently flatten it out into a circle until it is slightly wider than the pie dolly. Dust the pie dolly well with flour, centre it on top of the dough circle and then firmly press it down into the dough. The dough will rise up the sides of the dolly and puff out like an inflatable swimming ring. Lift the dolly out of the dough and dust it with more flour. Return the dolly to the centre of the dough and, cupping the edges of the dough in your hands, squeeze it up the dolly while at the same time turning and also pushing down on the dolly. Imagine a pottery wheel as you turn and squeeze, keeping the pastry as tight to the dolly as possible. Periodically, pause to lift out the dolly and dust with more flour to prevent the pastry from sticking to it. Keep working the pastry dough in this way until the wall of the pastry case is about 7–8cm in height and the base is 5mm thick.

Carefully remove the dolly from the pastry case and pack it with one of the balls of pork meat filling.

Repeat with the remaining 150g balls of dough until you have four pie cases filled with the pork meat filling. There should be a slight excess of pastry at the top of each case, so gently curl that outwards to form a collar.

Preheat the oven to 190°C fan/210°C/gas mark 6½.

Take the pastry lids out of the refrigerator. Wet the pie collars with a little water and lay the lids on top. To join, firmly press the collars and lids together. Crimp the edges (see page 32 for crimping technique) into the middle and then transfer the pies back onto the lined baking tray.

Using a skewer or the tip of a knife, make a small hole in the top of each pie to allow the steam to escape. Avoiding the base, brush the wall and lid of each pie with the egg wash and return the pies to the lined baking tray.

Place the tray in the preheated oven and bake the pies for 35 minutes or until the core temperature reads 70°C on a digital probe thermometer. If you don't have a probe thermometer, insert a metal skewer into the centre of a pie and leave it there for 10 seconds – when it comes out, the skewer should be piping hot. Remove the pies from the oven and leave to rest for 10 minutes before serving with mash and gravy.

To serve
Perfect Mash (see page 238)
Onion, Stout and Thyme Gravy
    (see page 254)

Equipment
7.5cm diameter pie dolly and
    digital probe thermometer

Sardine, Olive & Onion Tartlets

Based on the classic Pissaladière from France, in this dish the sweet, savoury
onions act as a foil to the oily sardines, while thyme continues the earthy flavour.
If you can't get fresh sardine fillets, use tinned and lay them flat rather than
curling them up.

SERVES 4

On a lightly floured surface, roll the pastry out to 5mm-thick in a 40cm x
30cm rectangle. Slide the rolled-out pastry onto a sheet of parchment paper.
Using the egg wash, brush a 2.5cm border all the way around the rectangle
of pastry and then crimp in the edges to form a frame (see page 32). Lifting
the parchment paper, slide the whole thing onto a baking tray and chill in the
refrigerator for 25 minutes.

Preheat the oven to 200°C fan/220°C/gas mark 7. While the pastry is chilling,
prepare the onions. Put a non-stick frying pan over a medium heat. Add the
vegetable oil to the pan and heat for 1 minute, then add the sliced onions and
¼ teaspoon salt. (The salt will draw the moisture from the onions and speed
up the cooking.) Stirring regularly with a wooden spoon, cook the onions for
10–15 minutes or until well browned and caramelised. If the onions are cooking
too quickly, turn the heat down. Scrape the onions out of the pan and onto a
plate and leave to cool while you prepare the pastry.

Remove the rolled-out pastry from the refrigerator. Brush the crimped pastry
edge with the remaining egg wash and prick the pastry inside the frame all
over with a fork, right up to the edges. Pop the tray into the preheated oven and
bake the pastry for 15 minutes. Remove the tray from the oven, lay a sheet of
parchment paper over the top of the pastry and fill the centre with just enough
baking beans to weigh down the middle. Return the pastry to the oven for a
further 10 minutes. Remove the tray from the oven and carefully lift out the
parchment paper with the baking beans. Set aside the pastry on the baking
tray and leave to cool, but leave the oven on.

Once the pastry has cooled, spread the cooked onions evenly across the base
of the tart. Season the sardines with salt and pepper, then roll up each fillet
into a tight coil. Nestle the sardines on their sides in the onions and intersperse
the olives to fill in the gaps.

Put the tart back into the hot oven for 8 minutes or until the sardines are just
cooked – they should be slightly firm and no longer translucent. Remove the
tray from the oven and carefully transfer the tart to a serving platter. Scatter
the fresh thyme leaves across the top of the tart and drizzle all over with the
olive oil. Serve while still warm from the oven.

300g rough puff pastry (see
  page 66, or shop-bought
  puff pastry)
1 egg yolk beaten with
  1 teaspoon of water,
  for brushing
20ml vegetable oil
4 medium Spanish onions,
  peeled and sliced
500g fresh sardine fillets,
  pin boned
120g pitted green olives,
  halved
3 thyme sprigs, leaves picked
10ml extra-virgin olive oil
sea salt and freshly ground
  black pepper

Leek & White Pudding Croquettes

The savoury flavours of white pudding, a traditional Scottish breakfast sausagemeat, combine with freshly grated nutmeg to make these melting croquettes so moreish. I prefer to leave the croquettes to cool for a few minutes so they aren't too hot to eat and you can enjoy the flavours, instead of juggling them around in your mouth.

MAKES 12

70g butter
½ leek, finely sliced
90g plain flour
550ml whole milk
150g white pudding, finely crumbled
¼ whole nutmeg, freshly grated
½ teaspoon table salt
a few good grinds of black pepper
2 eggs
100g panko breadcrumbs or plain white breadcrumbs
1 litre vegetable oil

Melt the butter in a saucepan over a low-medium heat. Add the sliced leek and cook for 2 minutes to soften. Add 60g of the flour and cook for a further 6 minutes, stirring continuously.

Warm 500ml of the milk in another pan or microwave. Add half the warm milk to the pan with the leeks and, stirring continuously, simmer until it thickens. Continuing to stir, add the rest of the warm milk and bring it back up to a simmer. Reduce the heat to low and continue to cook for 15 minutes or until the mixture is thick and stodgy. Take the pan off the heat, stir the crumbled white pudding through the mixture and then season with the nutmeg, salt and a good amount of freshly ground black pepper.

Line a baking tray with clingfilm. Pour the croquette mixture onto the tray, cover the surface with more clingfilm and allow to cool to room temperature. Once cool, chill in the refrigerator for 1½ hours.

When ready to cook, take the tray from the refrigerator and divide the mixture into 12 equal portions, each weighing around 45g. Dust your hands with flour and then roll the mixture into 12 neat cylinders.

Scatter the remaining flour over a plate, crack the eggs into a small bowl and beat with the remaining milk. Tip the breadcrumbs into a larger bowl with enough room to toss the croquettes. First, roll each croquette through the flour and then dust off any excess. Next, dip each croquette in the beaten egg, again shaking off any excess. Finally, transfer each croquette to the bowl of breadcrumbs and toss them a few times until they are evenly coated. Transfer to a baking tray.

Fill a heavy-based pan with the vegetable oil and heat to 180°C. When the oil has reached temperature, lower the croquettes into the oil and fry them for 3 minutes or until golden brown. Fry the croquettes in small batches, if necessary, to avoid overcrowding the pan. Using a slotted spoon, remove the croquettes from the hot oil and drain on paper towels before serving.

Devilled Kidney Vol-au-Vents

Did vol-au-vents ever go out of fashion? Not in my house, friends. The case can be used for so many canapés, there are endless options for this neat little basket! I got into offal quite late; being served tough kidneys at school was almost enough to put me off for life, but I was converted in my twenties and have never looked back.

--------------------------------- MAKES 5 ---------------------------------

First, make the vol-au-vent cases. Preheat the oven to 190°C fan/210°C/gas mark 6½ and line a baking sheet with parchment paper. Lightly dust the work surface with flour and then roll the pastry into a large square 5mm thick. Place onto the lined tray and chill in the refrigerator for 15 minutes.

Remove the tray from the refrigerator and cut ten discs from the pastry dough using an 8cm round cutter. Rearrange five of the discs on the lined tray so they are spaced a little apart and brush lightly with the egg wash. For the remaining discs, using a smaller 6cm round cutter, remove the centres and discard. Working quickly while the pastry is still cold, carefully lift these rings up and lay over the whole discs on the tray, fitting them neatly on top as collars. Brush the collars with the egg wash and, using a fork, prick the centres of the vol-au-vents (but not the collars). Bake in the preheated oven for 20 minutes until the pastry is puffed and golden. Transfer the vol-au-vent cases to a wire rack to cool.

Once cool, using a small sharp knife, carefully remove any pastry from the centre of each vol-au-vent case to expose a deep hole. Be gentle or you may break a hole through the bottom or the sides. Store in an airtight container while you make the filling.

Peel the membranes (very thin skins) from the kidneys and split them lengthways with a sharp knife. Using a pair of kitchen scissors, snip out the white membrane. Tip the flour onto a plate and coat the kidneys in the flour.

Heat the oil in a large frying pan over a high heat. Once the oil is shimmering, drop in the kidneys, shaking off any excess flour as you take them from the plate. Cook the kidneys on one side for 1 minute then turn over and cook for a further 1 minute on the other side.

Remove the pan from the heat and add the devilled butter, Worcestershire sauce and salt. Move the kidneys around the pan to help melt the butter for a further 1 minute until the kidneys are well coated.

Scatter three-quarters of the picked parsley leaves into the pan and stir through. Spoon the kidney mixture into the vol-au-vent cases, dividing it equally, and sprinkle the remaining parsley leaves over the top to decorate.

For the vol-au-vents
450g classic puff pastry (see page 63, or shop-bought)
plain flour, for dusting
1 egg beaten with 1 teaspoon water, for brushing

For the filling
10 lamb kidneys
15g plain flour
25ml vegetable oil
80g Devilled Butter (see page 252)
1 tablespoon Worcestershire sauce
1½ teaspoon table salt
20g flat-leaf parsley, leaves picked but not chopped

Equipment
8cm and 6cm round pastry cutters

'Nduja Stuffed Brioche

'Nduja is the spicy, smoked Italian pork salumi that combines so many good bits of the pig – offal, shoulder, tripe – all mixed with Calabrian chilli. It's so addictive that I have to stop myself adding it to everything. Stuffed inside a warm pillow of brioche, however, 'nduja feels at home in this rich but incredibly light type of bread. For this recipe you will need small brioche moulds, which are easily available online. Try to get the non-stick ones, if you can.

MAKES 8

160g spreadable 'nduja
  sausage
10g butter, softened
400g brioche dough
  (see page 72)
1 egg yolk, beaten with
  2 teaspoons milk
3g black poppy seeds
sea salt

Equipment
8 small brioche moulds
  (7–8cm diameter)

With floured hands, divide the 'njdua sausage into 20g portions and roll into balls. Place on a small tray lined with parchment paper and freeze for 1½ hours or until hard.

Lightly brush eight small brioche moulds with the softened butter.

Weigh out the brioche dough and divide it into 50g portions. On a lightly floured surface, roll each piece of dough into a ball and then flatten into a disc approximately 8–10cm in diameter.

One by one, take the 'njdua from the freezer and encase them in the brioche dough discs, pinching the dough together around the 'nduja to seal. Roll each ball between your palms until the surface is perfectly smooth. Place one ball into each of the buttered brioche moulds.

Place the moulds on a baking tray and leave somewhere warm (such as inside an airing cupboard or on a shelf above a radiator as the dough won't rise when it is cold), and leave to prove for 2 hours.

Preheat the oven to 200°C fan/220°C/gas mark 7.

Lightly brush the tops of the brioche with the egg wash and then sprinkle a pinch of poppy seeds and a little sea salt over each. Place the moulds on the tray in the preheated oven and bake for 15 minutes, then lower the heat to 180°C fan/200°C/gas mark 6 for a further 5 minutes or until a skewer inserted into the brioche bun comes out clean.

Remove the brioche from the oven, turn them out of the moulds and allow to rest on a wire cooling rack for 5 minutes before serving while still warm.

Haggis Scotch Egg

A well-made Scotch egg with a warm, jammy yolk, juicy forcemeat and crispy breadcrumb coating is a thing of beauty. A near perfect snack, the Scotch egg can be a vehicle for so many variations on the original recipe. This is one of my favourites. The flavours are simple and clean, relying purely on quality ingredients being handled with a little care. If the idea of eating haggis has previously felt intimidating, this is a great way to try it and then, inevitably, fall deeply in love with it.

--- MAKES 4 ---

Place the sausagemeat in a large bowl and crumble in the haggis. Add the rosemary, sea salt and grind in a little white pepper, then mix well. Divide the mixture into four equal balls, each weighing 80g, and chill in the refrigerator.

Meanwhile, fill a small saucepan with enough water to cover four of the eggs (but don't actually add the eggs) and bring to the boil. Fill a large bowl with iced water and keep it close by. Carefully lower 4 eggs into the boiling water with a spoon, making sure you don't crack them on the base of the pan, and boil for 6 minutes. Remove the eggs from the pan using a slotted spoon and transfer to the bowl of iced water. Leave the eggs to cool for 10 minutes and then once cool enough to handle, peel the shells from the eggs and set aside to dry on paper towels.

Take three bowls. Put the flour into the first bowl, crack the remaining egg into the second bowl and beat it with the milk, then place the breadcrumbs into the final bowl, lightly crushing some of the crumbs in your hands for texture.

Flatten out the sausagemeat balls and wrap them in an even layer around the boiled eggs, making sure each egg is snugly wrapped in the meat. Roll each meat-wrapped egg in the flour and then dust off any excess. Next, dip the floured eggs in the beaten egg. Finally, coat each egg in the breadcrumbs, making sure they are well covered. Leave the eggs resting on the breadcrumbs in the bowl until ready to cook.

Preheat the oven to 180°C fan/200°C/gas mark 6. Fill a heavy-based pan with the vegetable oil and heat to 180°C (use a digital probe thermometer to check the temperature). When the oil has reached 180°C, lower the eggs into the oil and fry them for 1 minute 30 seconds or until golden brown. Using a slotted spoon, remove the eggs from the hot oil and place on paper towels to drain. Transfer the fried Scotch eggs to a baking tray and bake in the preheated oven for 5 minutes. Remove the Scotch eggs from the oven and leave to rest for 2 minutes before swiftly cutting them in half with a serrated knife for a clean cut through and serving while still warm.

160g good-quality pork
    sausagemeat
160g haggis
2 rosemary sprigs,
    finely chopped
½ teaspoon sea salt
white pepper
5 medium organic eggs,
    at room temperature
50g plain flour
50ml semi-skimmed milk
150g panko breadcrumbs or
    plain white breadcrumbs
1 litre vegetable oil

VEGETABLE PIES

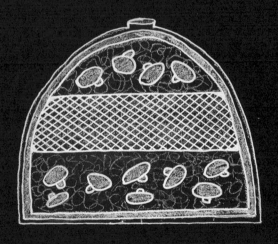

Moroccan Chickpea & Feta Pie

Probably the fastest pie in this book, this spiced chickpea and feta pie is also one of the tastiest. The crunchy filo provides a great contrast in texture to the soft filling beneath and looks deliciously dramatic when placed on the table.

SERVES 4

20ml light olive oil
2 Spanish onions, peeled
  and sliced
2 garlic cloves, peeled and
  finely sliced
1 teaspoon ras el hanout
1 teaspoon harissa paste
200g tinned chopped tomatoes
1 x 280g jar marinated
  chargrilled peppers, drained
  and sliced
1 x 400g tin chickpeas, drained
  and rinsed
150g feta cheese, broken into
  2cm chunks
½ bunch of mint,
  roughly chopped
½ bunch of flat-leaf parsley,
  roughly chopped
5 filo pastry sheets
light olive oil spray
sea salt

Equipment
large tagine or ovenproof dish

Preheat the oven to 180°C fan/200°C/gas mark 6.

Warm the olive oil in a frying pan over a medium heat. Add the sliced onions and garlic and gently sauté for 15 minutes or until soft. Add the ras el hanout and harissa paste and continue cooking for 1 minute. Stir in the tinned tomatoes and cook for a further 10 minutes, until the tomato sauce has thickened. Add the peppers and chickpeas, season and then set aside to cool a little.

Gently fold the feta, mint and parsley into the pie filling and spoon the mixture into a large tagine or ovenproof dish.

One at a time, lay the filo sheets on a chopping board and lightly coat them with the olive oil spray and a sprinkling of salt. Arrange the oiled filo sheets on the top of the pie filling, scrunching them up for added texture and height.

Place the dish in the preheated oven and bake the pie for 20 minutes, turning the dish around halfway through the cooking time so that the filo colours evenly.

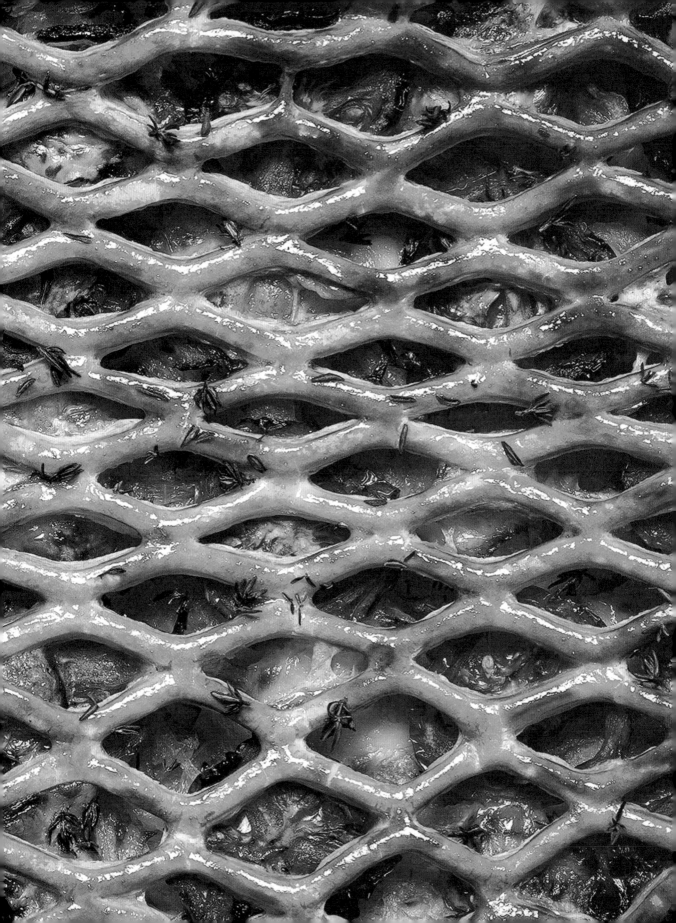

Tomato, Goats' Cheese & Onion Lattice

Served with a simple light salad and a chilled white wine, this tart is just as good
eaten at room temperature as it is piping hot. .

SERVES 4

Preheat the oven to 150°C fan/170°C/gas mark 3. Slice four of the tomatoes
into three thick slices each and then roughly cut the remaining tomatoes
into odd shapes – aim for five or six pieces from each. Line a baking tray with
parchment paper and lay the tomatoes evenly spaced over the tray. Place the
tray in the oven and roast the tomatoes for 25 minutes or until semi-dried.
Remove the tray from the oven and set aside for the tomatoes to cool.

Heat the olive oil in a frying pan over a medium heat. Add the onions and garlic
with half of the salt then gently sauté for 15 minutes or until soft. Remove the
pan from the heat and place alongside the tomatoes to cool.

Line a large baking tray with parchment paper. On a lightly floured surface,
roll the pastry out to a 40cm x 35cm rectangle. Slide the rolled-out pastry onto
the lined tray and chill in the refrigerator for 15 minutes (or 10 minutes in the
freezer). Once chilled, remove the tray from the refrigerator. Cut one 40cm x
12cm strip off the pastry and put this strip back into the refrigerator (this will
form the lattice later). Take the remaining 40cm x 23cm rectangle of pastry,
which will be the base of the tart. Leaving a 3cm border clear all around the
edge, spread the cooled onions and garlic evenly over the pastry.

Put the semi-dried tomatoes in bowl with the olive oil, remaining salt and half
the thyme, toss together and then scatter over the onions. Crumble the goats'
cheese into small chunks and scatter between the tomatoes.

Lightly brush the 3cm pastry border with the egg wash. Remove the reserved
pastry strip from the refrigerator. Using a lattice roller or the hand-cutting
technique (see page 33 for photograph), cut a lattice lengthways into the pastry
strip. Gently easing out the lattice, stretch the strip until the edges are aligned
with the egg-washed edges of the pastry base and the filling is covered. Crimp
over the pastry base onto the lattice (see page 32) and return to the refrigerator
for 15 minutes.

Preheat the oven to 180°C fan/200°C/gas mark 6. Remove the tart from the
refrigerator and gently brush the lattice with the remaining egg wash until well
coated. Scatter the remaining thyme leaves over the tart. Place the tray in the
hot oven and bake the tart for 25–30 minutes or until the pastry is golden all
over and the base is crispy. Slice at the table just before serving.

8 vine-ripened plum tomatoes
20ml olive oil
6 small sweet white onions
   (around 500g), peeled and
   thinly sliced
1 garlic clove, peeled and
   thinly sliced
½ teaspoon table salt
500g rough puff pastry (see
   page 66, or shop-bought
   puff pastry)
20ml extra-virgin olive oil
3 thyme sprigs, leaves picked
150g goats' cheese
1 egg yolk beaten with
   1 teaspoon water,
   for brushing

Beet Wellington

I always wanted to create an outstanding vegetarian wellington, one that proudly stands shoulder-to-shoulder with the beef wellington served in the Holborn Dining Room. This was the result. Unlike the beef version, which benefits from a two-day process, this vegetarian wellington is best made on the day of eating because the beetroot start to stain the squash after a while and you lose a little of the beautiful colour contrast when cut through. We added some North African spices to the squash to lift it a little and add another dimension of flavour.

--- SERVES 6 ---

500g rough puff pastry (see page 66, or shop-bought puff pastry)
3 egg yolks beaten with 1 teaspoon water, for brushing
1 tablespoon dukkah
pinch of sea salt

For the filling
5 large red beetroot
1 cinnamon stick
2 teaspoons cumin seeds
1 large butternut squash, peeled, deseeded and cut into 3cm dice
2 garlic cloves, unpeeled but crushed
30ml olive oil
1 teaspoon harissa paste
1 teaspoon ras el hanout
bunch of flat-leaf parsley, roughly chopped
sea salt and freshly ground black pepper

For the minted yoghurt
250g strained Greek yoghurt
bunch of fresh mint leaves, roughly chopped
lemon juice, to taste

First, prepare the beetroot. Fill a large pan with water and add plenty of salt – the water should taste as salty as seawater. Submerge the beetroot in the water and add the cinnamon stick and cumin seeds. Bring to the boil over a high heat and then lower to a gentle simmer and cook the beetroot for 2–3 hours or until soft enough to poke a skewer through the centre.

Meanwhile, prepare the squash. Preheat the oven to 200°C fan/220°C/gas mark 7. Put the diced squash and crushed garlic in a roasting tray, rub with the olive oil and sprinkle with salt. Place the tray in the preheated oven and roast the squash for 20 minutes, stirring with a spatula halfway through the cooking time so everything colours evenly.

Remove the tray from the oven, turn off the heat and transfer the squash to a food processor. Squeeze the roasted garlic cloves from their skins and add to the squash along with the harissa paste, ras el hanout and parsley. Pulse to a rough consistency, add seasoning to taste and then set aside to cool.

When the beetroot are cooked, remove from the pan with a slotted spoon and leave to steam. Once cool, rub the skin and any roots off the beetroot.

Line a large baking tray with parchment paper. On a lightly floured surface, roll the pastry out to a 40cm x 30cm rectangle. Slide the rolled-out pastry onto the lined tray and chill in the refrigerator for 15 minutes.

Remove the tray from the refrigerator. Dust off any excess flour from the surface of the rolled-out pastry and then brush liberally with the egg wash.

...continued on page 113

With one long edge of the pastry facing you, spread one-third of the squash mixture over the bottom third of the pastry rectangle, leaving a 2cm border around the edges. Trim a little from the bottom of each beetroot so they sit flat. Next, trim enough from two sides of each beetroot so they sit flush in a line together. Lay the beetroot in a line down the centre of the squash mixture, placing them tightly together with their flat bottoms facing upwards. Spread the remaining two-thirds of the squash mixture evenly all over the beetroot so they are completely covered.

Working away from you, roll the pastry over the filling into a cigar shape so the flat bottoms of the beetroot are facing downwards and the seam in the pastry is on the underside of the wellington. Leaving a 3cm overlap, trim away any excess pastry, reserving any trimmings for later use when decorating.

Carefully crimp down each end of the wellington (see page 32). Neaten the pastry so there is just enough to tuck back under the ends. Decorate the surface of the wellington however you prefer (see page 33). I cut out lots of leaf shapes in different sizes, which I then scored with lines radiating out from the centre. Brush the pastry all over with the egg wash and chill in the refrigerator for 30 minutes.

Preheat the oven to 180°C fan/200°C/gas mark 6.

Remove the wellington from the refrigerator, brush the pastry with egg wash one final time and sprinkle over the dukkah and a pinch of sea salt. Place the tray in the preheated oven and bake the wellington for 45 minutes or until the pastry is golden brown. Remove the tray from the oven and carefully slide the wellington onto a wooden board.

Tip the yoghurt into a small bowl and stir through the chopped mint. Add a squeeze of lemon juice to taste.

Using a serrated knife, cut the wellington into thick slices and serve the minted yoghurt alongside.

Cheesy Dauphinoise & Caramelised Onion Pie

This was the first vegetarian pie to make the transition from selling through the window of The Pie Room to being refined enough to be served in the Holborn Dining Room. At the heart of the pie is a warm, comforting embrace of a filling: creamy potato Dauphinoise oozing with melted cheese, caramelised onions and woody herbs, all contained within an elegant pastry crust.

SERVES 8–10

700g shortcrust pastry (see
    page 56, or shop-bought)
2 egg yolks beaten with
    2 teaspoons water,
    for brushing

For the potato Dauphinoise

1.5kg Maris Piper
    potatoes, peeled
500ml double cream
500ml semi-skimmed milk
6 rosemary sprigs, leaves
    picked and finely chopped
¼ bunch thyme, leaves picked
    and finely chopped
3 garlic cloves, peeled and
    finely chopped
20g table salt
200g strong Cheddar cheese,
    grated

For the caramelised onions

20ml vegetable oil
10g unsalted butter
3 large onions, peeled and
    thinly sliced
pinch of salt

Equipment

deep 25cm round
    ovenproof dish

First, make the potato Dauphinoise. Using a mandoline or sharp knife, slice the potatoes into 2–3mm thick slices. Put the cream, milk, rosemary, thyme, garlic and salt together in a wide-bottomed saucepan and gently warm over a low heat. Drop the potato slices into the pan, increase the heat and bring up to a gentle simmer. Using a spatula, continuously move the potatoes around to stop them from sticking to the base of the pan and cook for 3–4 minutes. Strain the potatoes, reserving the cooking liquid in a bowl.

Heat the vegetable oil and butter in a frying pan over a low–medium heat. Add the onions to the pan with a pinch of salt and sauté for 15 minutes or until caramelised and well browned.

Preheat the oven to 180°C fan/200°C/gas mark 6.

Line a deep 25cm round ovenproof dish with parchment paper. Lay one-third of the cooked potato slices in the base of the dish, scatter over half of the grated cheese and pour in one-third of the reserved cooking liquid. Using another one-third of the potato slices, lay them in a second layer, then spread all the caramelised onions across the surface and scatter over the remaining cheese. Next, place the remaining potato slices in a final layer and pour another one-third of the reserved cooking liquid over the top. Place a sheet of parchment paper over the top of the potato Dauphinoise and bake in the preheated oven for 35 minutes.

Remove the dish from the oven, lift off the parchment paper and pour the remaining cooking liquid over the potato Dauphinoise. Lower the oven temperature to 170°C fan/190°C/gas mark 5 and continue cooking for a further 20 minutes or until the potatoes are soft when the tip of a knife is inserted. Rather than being dry, there should still be quite a lot sauce. Place the dish on a wire cooling rack and leave the potato Dauphinoise to cool completely. Once cool, place the potato Dauphinoise in the refrigerator and chill for at least 1 hour.

...continued on page 117

Line a large baking tray with parchment paper.

Divide the pastry dough into two equal halves and place one half back in the refrigerator. On a lightly floured surface, roll the other half of the pastry out to a 5mm thick circle. Trim the pastry circle to 35cm in diameter, slide it onto the lined baking tray and chill in the refrigerator for 10 minutes.

Remove the pastry base and the potato Dauphinoise from the refrigerator. Loosen the parchment paper around the edges of the potato Dauphinoise and then quickly flip it over onto the pastry base.

On a lightly floured surface, roll out the remaining pastry dough to a 5mm thick circle large enough to cover the top and sides of the potato Dauphinoise. Carefully lay the rolled-out pastry over the potatoes and press it against and down the sides to join with the pastry base. Following the edge of the base, trim away any excess pastry, reserving any trimmings for decorating.

Decorate the surface of the pie however you prefer (see page 33). I cut out lots of leaf shapes in different sizes, which I then scored with lines radiating out from the centre, and placed over the pie top. I also added a plaited braid around the side of the pie. Brush the pastry all over with the egg wash and chill in the refrigerator for 30 minutes.

Meanwhile, preheat the oven to 180°C fan/200°C/gas mark 6.

Place the tray in the preheated oven and bake the pie for 45 minutes or until the pastry is golden brown.

Remove from the oven and, using a serrated knife, cut the pie into generous slices and serve while still warm.

Curried Cauliflower & Potato Pasties

These pasties are as wholesome eaten cold as they are hot and a great picnic item to take on a day out. They rarely make it as far as my picnic basket, though, as I'm forever eating them piping hot out of the oven – they're the main reason why I constantly have a burnt mouth. Add just a spoonful of mango chutney from a jar on the side for complete perfection.

— SERVES 4 —

800g hot water crust pastry
   (see page 59)
1 egg yolk beaten with
   1 teaspoon water,
   for brushing
mango chutney, to serve
sea salt

For the filling
2 tablespoons vegetable oil
1 teaspoon black
   mustard seeds
1 Spanish onion, peeled and
   thinly sliced
500g floury potatoes, peeled
   and cut into 1cm chunks
1 garlic clove, peeled and
   finely chopped
30g fresh ginger, peeled and
   finely chopped
2 green chillies, deseeded and
   finely chopped
1 teaspoon ground turmeric
1 teaspoon garam masala
2 plum tomatoes,
   roughly chopped
1 whole cauliflower, cut
   into florets
½ lime

To make the filling, warm 1 tablespoon of the oil in a large frying pan over a medium heat. Add the mustard seeds and let sizzle for 30 seconds. Add the onions and a pinch of salt and cook for 10–15 minutes until just starting to colour. Add the potatoes, garlic, ginger, chillies and spices, and cook for a further 5 minutes before adding the tomatoes and 100ml of water. Simmer for a further 15 minutes or until the potatoes are just cooked and the sauce has thickened.

Meanwhile, preheat the oven to 220°C fan/240°C/gas mark 9.

Rub the cauliflower florets all over with the remaining oil and scatter across a roasting tray. Place the tray in the preheated oven and roast the cauliflower for 15 minutes until softened and coloured.

Lower the oven temperature to 200°C fan/220°C/gas mark 7.

Add the cauliflower to the potato mixture, squeeze in the juice of half a lime, season to taste and then set aside to cool.

Divide the pastry dough into four equal balls. On a lightly floured surface, roll out each ball to a 1cm thick circle. Divide the filling mixture equally between the pastry discs, spooning it onto one half of each disc. Fold over the other half of each pastry disc to cover the filling and crimp the edges together (see page 32).

Line a baking tray with parchment paper. Place the pasties on the lined tray, brush the surface of the pastry all over with the egg wash and add a sprinkle of sea salt. Place the tray in the hot oven and bake the pasties for 25 minutes or until the pastry is golden brown. Serve either while still warm or at room temperature with a spoonful of mango chutney.

Red Onion, Carrot & Hazelnut Tatin

A pretty meal of balanced flavours, with the tarragon lifting the earthiness of the carrots and onion and the balsamic providing a little acidity to counteract the sweetness. This tarte tatin can be served for either lunch or dinner. If you have a lot of people coming around, it also makes a knockout vegetarian side dish for a banquet. Be really quite careful flipping over the pan at the end of the cooking – remember to use a cloth on the handle as it will have just come out of the oven.

SERVES 2–3

Preheat the oven to 210°C fan/230°C/gas mark 8.

Peel the onions and cut them in half through the roots so they stay intact, then cut each half through the root again into four wedges.

Place the carrot chunks and onion wedges in a large roasting tray, toss with the vegetable oil and salt then spread over the base of the tray. Place the tray in the preheated oven and roast the vegetables for 30 minutes or until they start to colour. Add the hazelnuts to the tray and roast for a further 5 minutes.

In a heavy ovenproof frying pan, warm the butter, sugar and balsamic vinegar until the sugar has dissolved. Bring the mixture to the boil and continue cooking until it has thickened enough to coat the back of a spoon. Add the roasted vegetables and nuts to the pan, toss well in the mixture and set aside to cool for 10 minutes.

On a lightly floured surface, roll out the pastry dough into a 1cm thick circle large enough to cover the frying pan. Bunch the vegetables and nuts together so there is a 2cm gap around the edge of the pan and then cover with the pastry, tucking it slightly under around the edge. Prick the pastry all over with a fork.

Place the frying pan in the hot oven and bake the tarte tatin for 20 minutes or until the pastry is puffed up and golden. Taking care to protect your hands with a heatproof cloth as the handle will be very hot, remove the pan from the oven. Place a large flat plate over the top of the pan and then quickly flip it over. Dress the top of the tarte tatin with the iced tarragon leaves and serve while warm.

3 red onions
4 large carrots, peeled and cut into 3cm chunks
2 tablespoons vegetable oil
½ teaspoon fine table salt
30g whole blanched hazelnuts
15g butter
15g caster sugar
2 teaspoons balsamic vinegar
150g rough puff pastry (see page 66, or shop-bought puff pastry)
10g tarragon, leaves picked and placed in iced water

Mac 'n' Cheese Pie

Taking out a slice of melting, gooey mac 'n' cheese from this pie is a magic moment.
It is the Gruyère cheese that provides this magic...

SERVES 6-8

700g shortcrust pastry (see
    page 56, or shop-bought)
5g butter
1 egg yolk beaten with
    1 teaspoon water,
    for brushing

For the filling
400g macaroni pasta
60g butter
45g plain flour
850ml whole milk, warmed
100g sundried tomatoes
100g strong Cheddar cheese,
    grated
80g Gruyère cheese, grated
10g thyme, leaves picked
1 teaspoon table salt
freshly ground black pepper

Equipment
24cm round springform cake tin

Line a large baking tray with parchment paper. On a lightly floured surface, roll one-third of the pastry out to a 5mm thick circle. Slide the rolled-out pastry onto the lined baking tray and chill in the refrigerator until needed.

Grease a 24cm round springform cake tin with the butter. Roll out the remaining two-thirds of the pastry to a 5mm thick circle. Line the greased tin with the rolled-out pastry, firmly pressing it into the base and sides. Leaving 3cm overhanging all the way round, trim the excess pastry around the edge of the tin, reserving the trimmings for decorating. Chill the pastry-lined tin in the refrigerator for 30 minutes (or 15 minutes in the freezer).

Next, make the filling. Cook the macaroni in plenty of salted water until tender. Drain the pasta and then rinse under cold running water to stop it cooking. Melt the butter in a large saucepan over a medium heat. Lower the heat a little, then add the flour and, stirring continuously, cook for 8 minutes, being careful not to brown the mixture. Add one-third of the milk and whisk into the flour mixture until it has thickened. Add the rest of the milk in thirds, each time bringing the sauce to a simmer until it has thickened and whisking to remove any lumps.

Using paper towels, pat dry the sundried tomatoes to remove any traces of oil. Roughly chop the tomatoes and add to the sauce along with the grated cheeses, thyme leaves, salt and lots of freshly ground black pepper. Take the pan off the heat. Stir the sauce until the cheeses are fully incorporated, then add the cooked pasta and mix well. Pour the macaroni cheese into a baking dish, cover with clingfilm and allow to cool to room temperature. Once cool, fill the pastry-lined tin with the macaroni cheese.

Preheat the oven to 190°C fan/210°C/gas mark 6½. Remove the tray from the refrigerator and cut the rolled-out pastry into a lid just large enough to fit the top of the pie with a slight overhang. Brush the 3cm overhang of the pastry base with the egg wash and carefully lay the lid over the top of the pie. Firmly press the outer edges of the pastry together. Crimp the edges of the lid (see page 32) and decorate the pie however you prefer (see page 33). Lightly brush the pastry all over with the egg wash.

Bake the pie for 45 minutes or until the pastry is golden brown and the core temperature is 70°C or above when tested with a digital probe thermometer. Serve while still warm and the macaroni cheese is all gooey and stringy.

FISH & SHELLFISH PIES

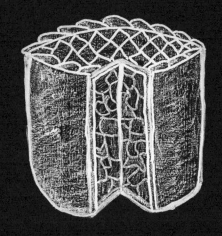

Smoked Haddock & Sweetcorn Chowder Pot Pies

These are great individual pies to make ahead of time, ready to pop in the oven for an easy dinner. When you break through the puff pastry lid, the mouth-watering aroma of the smoked haddock hits you, and I think the sweet flavour of the corn balances the smokiness of the fish beautifully.

MAKES 4

To make the chowder, pour the fish stock into a small pan, add the diced potatoes and bring to a simmer over a low heat. Cook the potatoes until just tender, but not falling apart. Drain the potatoes and reserve the fish stock.

Heat the butter in a medium pan over a medium–low heat, add the diced onion and cook for 8 minutes until soft. Remove the onion with a slotted spoon, allowing any butter to drain back off into the pan and set aside in a bowl. Add the flour and spices, reduce the heat to low and cook for a further 8 minutes, stirring continuously. Add 100ml of the milk to the butter and flour mixture and whisk continuously until the sauce has thickened. Add another 100ml of the milk and whisk again to remove any lumps. Repeat with the remaining 100ml of milk.

Add the reserved fish stock to the pan, increase the heat and bring to a boil, whisking continuously until smooth. Whisk in the double cream. Add the cooked potatoes, onion, diced haddock, sweetcorn kernels and chopped parsley, season with the salt and then stir to mix well. Ladle the chowder into four individual ovenproof bowls. Allow the chowder to cool to room temperature and then chill in the refrigerator until cold.

Meanwhile, prepare the puff pastry lids. On a lightly floured surface, roll out the pastry to 5mm thick. Cut out four discs from the pastry, each 5cm wider in diameter than the lip of the ovenproof bowls. Slide the discs onto a tray and chill in the refrigerator for 30 minutes. Set aside any leftovers for decoration.

Preheat the oven to 190°C fan/210°C/gas mark 7. Remove the cold bowls of chowder from the refrigerator and place on a baking tray. Brush the lip of each bowl with egg wash and 2.5cm down the sides. Place a pastry lid centrally on top of each bowl, firmly pressing the edges of the disc against the sides of the bowl all the way round. Egg wash the tops of the pastry lids and add any decoration that you like. Place the tray in the preheated oven and bake for 25 minutes or until the pastry has risen and is golden in colour. Before serving, check the pot pies are hot inside. Insert a digital probe thermometer into the centre of a pie – the temperature should be 80°C or above. If necessary, return to the oven for a further 5 minutes or until the chowder comes to temperature. Serve the pot pies while hot along with some slices of crusty bread.

400g rough puff pastry (see page 66 or shop-bought puff pastry)
1 egg yolk beaten with 1 teaspoon water

For the chowder
500ml fish stock
250g King Edward potatoes, peeled and cut into 1.5cm dice
30g butter
1 Spanish onion, peeled and finely diced
15g plain flour
1 pinch of cayenne pepper
1 pinch of ground mace
300ml whole milk
20ml double cream
250g skinless smoked haddock fillet, cut into 1.5cm dice
250g drained sweetcorn kernels from a can
40g flat-leaf parsley, leaves picked and roughly chopped
½ teaspoon salt
slices of crusty bread, to serve

Equipment
4 individual ovenproof bowls

The Ultimate Fish Pie

Tony Fleming, my old boss, once described the perfect fish pie to me: he said that if a fish pie is not bubbling down the sides of the dish and browned on the surface, it is not a good one. At the time, I was working for Tony in a fine-dining restaurant where the food presentation was all about accuracy, finesse and clean lines and so the look of the fish pie went against the grain of everything else we did there. But Tony was right. A fish pie should never be de-constructed. It should never be neat and tidy. It should always be homely, rustic and even messy – that is what makes it so appealing and gets the taste buds firing when it arrives on the dining table.

SERVES 6

500ml whole milk

300ml double cream

300g skinless cod fillets, cut into 2.5cm dice

200g skinless salmon fillet, cut into 2.5cm dice

200g skinless smoked haddock fillet, cut into 2.5cm dice

150g peeled raw tiger prawns

60g butter

60g plain flour

300g frozen peas, thawed

30g capers

30g chives, finely chopped

30g flat-leaf parsley, leaves picked and chopped

1 tablespoon Dijon mustard

¾ teaspoon table salt

For the potato topping

1.2kg King Edward potatoes, peeled and quartered

200ml whole milk

100ml double cream

60g butter

2 egg yolks, beaten

¾ teaspoon table salt

50g Cheddar cheese, grated

Equipment

ovenproof dish (approx. 25cm long and 3cm deep)

Preheat the oven to 180°C fan/200°C/gas mark 6.

To make the potato topping, put the potatoes in a pan and add enough salted water just to cover them. Bring to the boil, then reduce the heat and simmer until the potatoes are very tender. Add the milk, double cream and butter to the pan and mash together with the potatoes until smooth. Add the egg yolks with the table salt and mix until well incorporated.

Pour the milk and cream into a medium pan and bring to a simmer. Drop the diced fish and peeled prawns into the simmering milk and cream and poach for 2 minutes. Drain the fish, reserving the poaching liquid in a bowl.

Wipe out the pan and add the butter, bring it to a bubble over a medium heat and then whisk in the flour. Reduce the heat to low and cook for 8 minutes, whisking continuously. Add half of the reserved poaching liquid and bring back up to a simmer, whisking continuously to prevent any lumps from forming. Add the remaining poaching liquid and cook until thick and smooth. Add the peas, capers, chives, parsley, mustard and table salt and mix well. Return the drained fish to the pan and lightly fold into the sauce, being careful not to break up the fish.

Spoon the pie mixture into a deep ovenproof dish and level the surface. Spread the mashed potato topping over the pie mixture, taking it right to the edges of the dish, and then ruffle the top with a fork to create texture. Scatter the grated cheese evenly over the surface of the pie.

Place the dish in the preheated oven and bake the pie for 30 minutes or until the sauce is bubbling up at the sides and the potato topping has a crispy, golden crust.

Salmon & Minted Pea Filo Parcels

A really quick dinner that is great to get the family involved in the pastry folding process. Inside crisp, buttery pastry, the minted peas marry with the flavour of the salmon, making for a tasty bite. Pop some vine cherry tomatoes on the roasting tray, dressed in just a little olive oil and salt, about ten minutes before the parcels are ready and you will have a lovely meal in very little time.

SERVES 4

Preheat the oven to 190°C fan/210°C/gas mark 7 and line a baking tray with parchment paper.

To make the pea purée, bring a medium pan of salted water to the boil, drop in the peas, allow the water to return to the boil and cook for 2 minutes. Drain the peas, put half in a food processor with the melted butter, pulse to a coarse purée and transfer to a bowl. Refresh the other half of the peas in iced water, strain and then stir through the puréed peas with the mint and the salt. Set aside to cool.

Cut each salmon fillet diagonally into two right-angled triangles. Lay one sheet of the filo on a board with one shorter edge facing you. Lightly brush with melted butter. Lay one triangle of salmon in the bottom third of the pastry so the long diagonal edge runs from the bottom right corner and then up and across the left. Trim the pastry along both long edges so it is 1cm wider than the salmon. Discard the trimmings.

Spread 2 tablespoons of the pea mixture over the salmon. Slide your hand under the pastry sheet and tightly fold the bottom left corner diagonally over and across the salmon to the right. Next, fold the salmon directly upwards to make a tight horizontal fold, and then make the third fold diagonally to the left by folding the salmon across from the bottom right to the top left. Continue in this way, folding the salmon up and then diagonally across, until you have a neat triangular pastry-wrapped parcel. Put the parcel on the lined tray.

Repeat with the remaining portions of salmon, the pea purée and more filo pastry sheets. (Any leftover pea purée can be frozen and then reheated to serve with fish and chips at a later date.)

Give the pastry parcels a final brush of melted butter. Place the tray in the preheated oven and bake the parcels for 20 minutes or until the pastry is crisp and golden. Serve with roasted vine cherry tomatoes.

2 salmon centre-cut fillets
(250g each), skin removed
4 filo pastry sheets
(20cm x 30cm each)
20g butter, melted

For the minted pea purée
500g frozen peas, thawed
30g butter, melted
30g mint, leaves picked and
roughly chopped
½ teaspoon table salt

Smoked Eel, Potato & Parsley Quiche

The ingredients in this quiche scream Britishness to me and together they remind me of both the St. John and Quo Vadis restaurants in London. I adore smoked eel; it's incredibly moreish. Never serve anything too overpowering with smoked eel, only simple things that help perk it up and allow it to stand proud.

───────────────── SERVES 6–8 ─────────────────

400g shortcrust pastry (see
    page 56 or shop-bought)
5g butter, softened
1 egg yolk, for glazing
salad leaves, to serve
creamed horseradish, to serve

For the filling

250g new potatoes
5 medium free-range eggs
250ml whole milk
250ml double cream
350g boneless, skinless
    smoked eel fillet, cut
    into 1cm dice
50g flat-leaf parsley, leaves
    picked and roughly chopped
80g mature Cheddar,
    finely grated
fine table salt freshly ground
    black pepper

Equipment

24cm diameter loose-
    bottomed tart tin

On a lightly floured surface, roll out the pastry dough into a large disc 1cm thick then place on a parchment-lined tray to rest in the refrigerator for 30 minutes or in the freezer for 15 minutes.

Place the potatoes in a small pan and cover with cold water. Add a little salt, bring to the boil over a high heat and cook until the potatoes are just tender. Drain the potatoes and set aside to cool.

Grease the inside of the tart tin with the butter then line it with the chilled disc of pastry. Press the pastry firmly against the sides of the tin and into the corners. Using a fork, prick the base of the pastry case all over. Put it back in the refrigerator for 20 minutes.

Preheat the oven to 190°C fan/210°C/gas mark 6½. Once rested, trim any excess pastry from the top edge of the tin. Line the pastry case with baking parchment and fill with ceramic baking beans. Bake in the preheated oven for 15 minutes. Remove the baking beans and parchment from the pastry case and return to the oven for a further 20 minutes. If any small cracks have appeared in the pastry, brush the egg yolk over them and return to the oven for 1 minute to set.

Meanwhile, whisk together the eggs, milk and cream in a large mixing bowl until well combined. Add ½ teaspoon of salt and a few good twists of black pepper. Peel the skins from the potatoes and cut into quarters . Add to the mix with the eel and parsley.

Set the tart tin on a baking tray. Give the filling a good stir and pour it into the pastry case, making sure the eel and potatoes are evenly distributed. Place the tray in the hot oven and bake the tart for 15 minutes. Scatter the grated cheese over the top of the quiche and cook for a further 15 minutes or until the cheese is golden. The tart should have a very slight wobble but not be liquid.

Allow the quiche to cool in the tin for 10 minutes. Carefully remove the quiche from the tin by setting it over a bowl smaller than the hole in the base and allowing the sides of the tin to drop away. Serve the quiche, either warm or at room temperature, with a lightly dressed salad and a dollop of creamed horseradish.

Hot & Sour Curried Cod Pie

Breaking through the flaky pastry on the top of this pie releases all of the curry aromas at the dinner table. The cod is interchangeable with other firm-fleshed white fish, like hake or coley, and the tamarind can be swapped for the juice of half a lime if you find it difficult to get hold of. As this pie is a complete meal in itself, I wouldn't serve it with rice, but if you can't have curry without it, then I'm not going to stop you.

SERVES 2–3

Sprinkle the cod all over with sea salt and set aside for 15 minutes. Rinse the cod well in cold water, pat dry with kitchen paper and set aside in the refrigerator.

Heat the oil in a large frying pan for 1 minute over a medium heat. Add the mustard seeds, sizzle for 30 seconds, then add the onions and a pinch of salt and cook for 10 minutes until the onions are well cooked and starting to colour. Add the garlic and chillies and cook for a further 1 minute before adding the dry spices and cooking for a further 5 minutes. Add the tomatoes and tamarind paste and cook for a further 10 minutes. Stir in the coriander and set aside to cool.

Once cool, add the cod to the filling mixture and spoon into a shallow ovenproof dish that just fits the mixture.

On a lightly floured surface, roll out the pastry dough into a disc 1cm thick. Brush the outside lip of the dish with a little of the egg wash and lay the pastry disc over, pressing it well against the egg-washed lip. Trim off anything over a 2cm overlap with a small knife. Brush the pastry with the remaining egg and sprinkle over the fennel and sesame seeds and a touch of sea salt. Put into the refrigerator for 20 minutes.

Preheat the oven to 200°C fan/220°C/gas mark 7.

Place the dish in the preheated oven and bake the pie for 25 minutes or until golden. Serve with steamed broccoli tossed in a little butter and sprinkled with toasted almonds.

400g skinless, boneless cod fillet, diced into 2cm chunks
1 tablespoon vegetable oil
1 teaspoon black mustard seeds
2 Spanish onions, peeled and thinly sliced
1 garlic clove, peeled and finely chopped
2 green chillies, deseeded and finely chopped
1 teaspoon hot curry powder
½ teaspoon ground turmeric
1 teaspoon ground cumin
6 plum tomatoes, roughly chopped
2 tablespoons tamarind paste
20g coriander, stalks and leaves roughly chopped
300g rough puff pastry (see page 66 or shop-bought puff pastry)
pinch of fennel seeds
pinch of black sesame seeds
1 medium egg beaten with 1 tablespoon water
sea salt

To serve
broccoli florets
butter
flaked almonds, toasted

Equipment
shallow ovenproof dish

Baked Scallops with Green Lentils, Pancetta & Red Wine

A truly delicious way to prepare scallops, baking them in their shells sealed in a layer of puff pastry allows some of the seafood juices to be absorbed and plumps the scallops with flavour. This dish works as either a starter or a main course.

I serve one scallop per person for a starter, while for a main I accompany the two or three scallops with a bowl of buttery mashed potato. If you want them to stand proud on the plate, spoon a knob of mash onto the plate and sit the scallop shell on top. This is about as classical as cooking gets, so these scallops are best eaten while wearing a smoking jacket and monocle.

SERVES 6 AS A STARTER OR 2–3 AS A MAIN

150g dried green lentils

400g rough puff pastry (see page 66 or shop-bought puff pastry)

2 tablespoons mild olive oil

1 banana shallot, peeled and finely diced

1 large carrot, peeled and cut into 1cm dice

1 garlic clove, peeled and finely chopped

1 x 400g can chopped tomatoes

500ml beef stock

150ml red wine

150g diced pancetta

10g rosemary, leaves picked and finely chopped

5g thyme, leaves picked

6 medium–large scallops on the half shell

1 egg yolk beaten with 1 teaspoon water

sea salt

Put the lentils in a bowl, cover with cold water and leave to soak for 1 hour.

Line a baking tray with baking parchment. On a lightly floured surface, roll out the pastry dough into a rectangle 1cm thick. Using a scallop shell as a guide, cut six discs from the pastry roughly one-third larger than the scallop. Put the pastry discs on the lined tray and chill in the refrigerator. (Any pastry trimmings can be re-rolled or saved for another recipe.)

In a medium saucepan, warm 1 tablespoon of the oil over a medium heat. Add the diced shallot and carrot with a pinch of salt and cook for 5 minutes or until softened. Add the garlic and cook for a further 1 minute. Add the chopped tomatoes and cook for 10 minutes. Add the stock and wine, then bring to a simmer. Strain the soaked lentils and rinse under warm water. Add the lentils to the pan, stir through and bring back to a simmer.

Meanwhile, warm the remaining oil in a small frying pan over a medium heat. Add the diced pancetta and cook for 2–3 minutes until coloured. Strain the pancetta through a sieve and then add it to the pan with the lentils.

Cook the lentils until the stock and wine have reduced and the sauce has started to thicken. Taste the lentils; if they still have a bite then add a touch of water and cook for a little longer. When the lentils are cooked and the sauce is thick, season to taste. Add the rosemary and thyme leaves, then stir through. Spread the lentil mixture across a shallow bowl and leave to cool.

Using a dessertspoon, gently scrape away the scallop from the shell, keeping the spoon close to the shell to not lose any meat. If visible, remove any of the brown/grey skirt, but leave the orange roe on as it's super tasty.

Lightly rinse the scallops under cold water and then pat them dry with kitchen paper.

Turn the scallops shells over, dry their backs and brush with a little of the egg wash. Turn the shells back over, put 1 heaped tablespoon of the lentil mixture into each shell and then place the scallops on top. Fill the gaps around the scallops with more lentil mixture until level. Sprinkle a little sea salt on top of each scallop.

Place a pastry disc over each scallop and take the overlap around to the back of the shell, firmly pressing so it sticks to the egg-washed rear. Brush more egg wash over the surface of the pastry. Scrunch up a tea towel and place it on a tray, then nestle the scallop shells in the cloth to keep them horizontal. Put in the refrigerator to rest for 20 minutes.

Preheat the oven to 200°C fan/220°C/Gas Mark 7.

When ready to bake, remove the scallops from the refrigerator and lightly score the pastry to look like the original scallop shell. Place the tray in the preheated oven and bake the scallops for 20 minutes. Leave to cool for 5 minutes before serving.

MEAT & POULTRY PIES

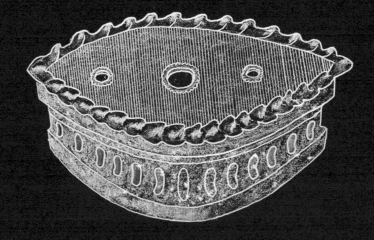

Chicken, Mushroom & Tarragon Pie

This pie holds a special place in the hearts of The Pie Room chefs, as it was the first pie we sold as a takeaway from The Pie Hole – our window straight onto the street in Holborn. Without fail, it is our biggest seller every day. This is one of those pies that people will ask you to make for them again and again, yet it is really simple to cook at home.

——————— SERVES 6 ———————

700g shortcrust pastry (see page 56, or shop-bought)
5g butter, softened
1 egg yolk beaten with 1 teaspoon water, for brushing

For the filling
800g chicken thighs
1 litre chicken stock
300ml dry cider
2 teaspoons table salt
400g button mushrooms, cleaned and halved
40g butter
30g plain flour
60ml double cream
1 tablespoon English mustard
25g tarragon, leaves picked and chopped

Equipment
fluted oval game pie mould (24cm long and 8cm deep)

Put the chicken thighs in a saucepan. Pour over the chicken stock and cider, then add 1 teaspoon of the table salt. Bring to a simmer over a medium heat and cook for 15 minutes. Add the mushrooms to the pan and cook for a further 5 minutes. Remove the pan from the heat and strain the stock through a colander into a second clean pan. Set aside the chicken and mushrooms to cool slightly. Once cool, slice each chicken thigh into three.

Place the pan of stock over a medium heat, skim any excess fat from the surface with a spoon every 10 minutes as it comes back to a simmer, and cook until the stock has reduced by half.

While the stock is reducing, prepare the pastry case. On a lightly floured surface, roll out the pastry to a 5mm thick large rectangle. Cutting diagonally from corner to corner, cut a pastry strip 20cm wide and at least 50cm long, squaring off the ends. Lay the pastry strip on a large piece of parchment paper, folding the pastry if necessary, and chill in the refrigerator until needed.

Unclip the pie mould and take it apart. Using the shape of the pie mould as a guide, cut out two ovals from the resulting triangles of pastry, reserving any trimmings for decoration.

Re-assemble the pie mould and secure it with the clips. Brush the inside of the mould with the softened butter. Remove the strip of pastry from the refrigerator, gently fold it into a loop and carefully place it inside the greased mould. Let the bottom 2cm of the pastry strip slide down onto the base of the mould and flatten down. Next, press the pastry strip against the sides of the mould following the fluted shape. There should be a substantial overhang of pastry at the top of the mould, which you can ease over the top edge by making small snips in the pastry at either pointed end of the mould. After pressing the sides in, make sure the seam where the two ends of the pastry strip meet is no more than a 2cm overlap. Trim any excess pastry with scissors, if necessary, then push the ends firmly together.

Take one of the pastry ovals, trim 1cm from all the way round the edge and lay it on the base of the mould. Push the pastry oval against the mould and into the pastry strip where it overlaps the base to join the two. Put the pastry-lined mould into the refrigerator with the remaining pastry oval and any trimmings for decoration and chill for 30 minutes.

Wipe clean the first pan. Put the butter and flour together in the pan and warm over a medium heat. When the butter starts to bubble, reduce the heat to low and cook for 6 minutes, stirring frequently. Gradually add the reduced stock to the butter and flour, one ladleful at a time, stirring well between each addition to stop any lumps from forming and allow the sauce to thicken. Continue until all the stock has been incorporated. Add the double cream and mustard to the sauce and bring it back to a simmer and then cook for a further 4 minutes. Taste and if necessary add more seasoning.

Fold the chicken pieces and mushrooms into the sauce and spread the pie filling mixture over a roasting tray to cool quickly. Once the pie filling has cooled to room temperature, pop the tray into the refrigerator for 10 minutes to cool further. Remove the tray from the refrigerator and fold the chopped tarragon into the pie filling.

Preheat the oven to 190°C fan/210°C/gas mark 6.

Remove the pastry-lined mould from the refrigerator. Spoon the chilled pie filling into the pastry case and level the surface. Lay the remaining pastry oval over the top of the filling and lightly brush with the egg wash. Crimp together the lid and sides of the pastry case (see page 32) so the pie is sealed all the way round. Lightly brush again with the egg wash, this time brushing the crimped edges too. Return the mould to the refrigerator and chill the pie for 20 minutes.

Remove the mould from the refrigerator and cut a 2cm hole in the middle of the pie lid to allow steam to escape. Decorate the top of the pie however you prefer (see page 33). Lightly brush the pastry all over with egg wash and then return to the refrigerator to chill for 20 minutes. When ready to bake, remove the pie from the refrigerator and brush again with the egg wash.

Place the mould on a rack in the centre of the preheated oven and bake the pie for 45 minutes or until the pastry is golden brown. Halfway through the cooking time, turn the tin around in the oven to ensure an even bake. Take the pie out of the mould and serve with some simple steamed broccoli.

Left to right:

Turkey, Stuffing & Cranberry Pie
(page 152) and Pork, Apricot &
Sage Picnic Pie (page 155)

Turkey, Stuffing & Cranberry Pie

A Christmas classic, this is a brilliant pie to serve when entertaining family and friends before the actual big day. This pie can be made the night before so that it has plenty of time to chill in the refrigerator and you can spend more time relaxing (or not) with your mother-in-law the next day.

───────────────────────── SERVES 6 ─────────────────────────

5g butter
800g shortcrust pastry (see
    page 56, or shop-bought)
1 egg yolk beaten with
    1 teaspoon water,
    for brushing

For the stuffing
100g butter
200g white onions,
    finely chopped
1 garlic clove, peeled
    and finely chopped
20g chopped sage
100g white breadcrumbs

For the filling
600g turkey breast, cut
    into 3cm dice
500g turkey mince
30g salt
100g dried cranberries
    (preferably sulphur-free)

Equipment
24cm non-stick loaf tin

Grease the loaf tin with the butter and line with a strip of parchment paper, allowing the ends to overhang. On a lightly floured surface, roll out one-third of the dough to a 5mm thick strip long enough to cover the top of the tin. Lay this on a tray and refrigerate until needed. Roll out the remaining dough into a large rectangle 5mm thick and use it to line the greased tin (see page 28). Reserve any trimming for decoration. Put the pastry-lined tin into the freezer for 15 minutes or until the dough has set hard.

Meanwhile, make the stuffing mixture. Melt the butter in a pan and add the onions and garlic, gently sautéing until just soft. Stir in the sage and breadcrumbs and set aside to cool.

Combine the turkey breast and mince, cranberries and salt together in a large bowl and mix well. Break the cooled stuffing into small nuggets and stir through the turkey and cranberry mixture.

Remove the pastry-lined tin from the freezer. Pack the pastry case with the filling mixture and level the surface. Lightly brush the overhanging edges of the pastry case with the egg wash. Lay the pastry lid on top of the pie and lightly brush with the egg wash. When the overhanging lip of the pastry case is pliable enough, firmly join the edges and crimp over onto the lid by at least 3cm (see page 32) so the pie is sealed all the way round. Lightly brush again with the egg wash, this time brushing the crimped edges too, and decorate however you prefer using the reserved pastry trimmings (see page 33). Make three small holes in the lid to allow steam to escape during cooking. Return the pie to the refrigerator and chill for 20 minutes.

Preheat the oven to 180°C fan/200°C/gas mark 6. Place the tin on a rack in the centre of the preheated oven and bake the pie for 1 hour or until the pastry is golden brown and the core temperature of the filling has reached at least 50°C on a digital probe thermometer. Halfway through the cooking time, turn the tin in the oven to ensure an even bake. Remove the pie from the oven and leave to cool in the tin and then place in the refrigerator to chill overnight.

Using the parchment paper, ease the pie out of the loaf tin. Cut the pie into thick slices with a serrated knife and then serve with more cranberry sauce.

Pork, Apricot & Sage Picnic Pie

This pie is the perfect summer picnic food. The three main ingredients here are made for each other: the sweet sharpness of the apricot lifting the flavour of the pork, while the sage rounds everything off.

SERVES 6-8

Grease the loaf tin with the butter and line with a strip of parchment paper, allowing the ends to overhang. On a lightly floured surface, roll out one-third of the dough to a 5mm thick strip long enough to cover the top of the tin. Lay this on a tray and refrigerate until needed. Roll out the remaining dough into a large rectangle 5mm thick and use it to line the greased tin (see page 28). Reserve any trimming for decoration. Put the pastry-lined tin into the freezer for 15 minutes or until the dough has set hard.

Finely mince the pork shoulder in a food processor. Place it in a large bowl, add the remaining ingredients for the meat farce and mix together, working it well with your hands. The mixture will start to become a little sticky.

Remove the pastry-lined tin from the refrigerator. Pack the pastry case with the meat farce and level the surface. Lightly brush the overhanging edges of the pastry with the egg wash. Lay the pastry lid on top of the pie and lightly brush with the egg wash. Firmly join the edges and crimp together (see page 32). Make a small hole in the centre of the lid for steam to escape. Lightly brush the top of the pie with the egg wash, brushing the crimped edges too, and decorate however you prefer using the reserved pastry trimmings (see page 33). Brush with egg wash one final time, return to the refrigerator and chill for 20 minutes.

Preheat the oven to 180°C fan/200°C/gas mark 6. Place the tin on a rack in the centre of the preheated oven and bake the pie for 1 hour or until the pastry is golden brown and the core temperature of the filling has reached at least 65°C on a digital probe thermometer. Halfway through the cooking time, turn the tin around in the oven to ensure an even bake. Remove the pie from the oven and leave to cool in the tin overnight.

The following day, make the jelly. Soak the gelatine in cold water for 5 minutes. Meanwhile, pour the cider into a pan and boil until reduced by half. Add the chicken stock and sage stalks to the pan and remove from the heat. Drain the gelatine and squeeze out any excess water. Add the gelatine to the stock and whisk until it is fully incorporated. Pass the jelly mixture through a sieve to ensure it is completely smooth, discarding the sage stalks. Using a small funnel, carefully pour the jelly mixture into the pie through the steam hole in the lid. Place the pie in the refrigerator for 1 hour to allow the jelly to set. Remove the pie from the tin and it is ready to serve.

5 butter
800g shortcrust pastry (see page 56, or shop-bought)
1 egg yolk beaten with 1 teaspoon water, for brushing

For the meat farce

1kg pork shoulder, skin removed
450g smoked streaky bacon, roughly chopped
100g dried apricots (preferably sulphur-free), roughly chopped
¼ bunch sage, leaves roughly chopped and stalks reserved for the jelly (see below)
1 teaspoon table salt
a large pinch of white pepper
5g white mustard seeds
10g butter, softened

For the jelly

6 gelatine leaves
100ml dry cider
300ml chicken stock
4 sage stalks

Equipment

24cm non-stick loaf tin

Beef Cheek & Kidney Suet Pudding

An absolute British classic that is unique in so many ways. Unusually, the pastry is steamed so that it becomes slightly crusty and flaky during the cooking process. Encasing a deeply flavoured savoury stew, this suet pudding is synonymous with quintessential British cookery.

─────────────── SERVES 4 ───────────────

½ quantity suet pastry (see page 70, but only make the dough once the pie filling is cooling and make sure the butter is in the freezer before you start)

5g butter, for greasing

For the filling

200g beef kidneys

500g beef cheek, cut into 4cm dice

20g plain flour

1 teaspoon table salt

30ml vegetable oil

1 Spanish onion, peeled and sliced

220ml dark ale

200ml beef stock

1 teaspoon Worcestershire sauce

10g thyme, leaves picked and chopped

10g rosemary, leaves picked and chopped

1 bay leaf

salt and freshly ground black pepper, to taste

Equipment

1.5-litre (2-pint) ovenproof pudding basin

First, make the filling. Using kitchen scissors, split the kidneys in half and snip out the white fat inside. Cut each half into quarters and place in a bowl. Add the diced beef cheek, flour and salt to the bowl and mix well until the flour has been absorbed.

Pour the oil into a large pan with a lid and place over a medium heat. When the oil is shimmering, add one-third of the meat and kidneys and cook until well browned. Using a slotted spoon, transfer the meat and kidneys to a plate and set aside. Repeat with the remaining beef, cooking it in two further batches. Do not clean or wipe out the pan.

Add the onion to the same pan, reduce the heat to low and, stirring with a wooden spoon, cook for 10 minutes until browning slightly. Add the ale, stock and Worcestershire sauce, scraping the bottom of the pan while stirring.

Return the meat and kidneys to the pan and then add the thyme, rosemary and bay leaf. Bring to a simmer, place the lid on the pan, and cook for 1 hour, stirring every 10–15 minutes. Cook for a further 1 hour with the lid off. Add a few good twists of freshly ground black pepper. Taste to check the seasoning and adjust with a little more salt, if necessary. Set aside to cool to room temperature.

While the filling is cooling, make and chill the suet pastry dough (see page 70).

When ready to cook the pudding, brush a 1.5-litre (2-pint) ovenproof pudding basin with the butter. Roll out three-quarters of the suet pastry dough to a 5mm thick large circle and use it to line the greased basin, allowing any excess to hang over the sides. Trim the overhanging pastry back to 2.5cm. Spoon the pudding filling into the pastry case, filling it to 2cm below the rim.

...continued on page 158

Roll out the remaining dough to a circle wide enough to sit on top of the basin and meet the sides. Lay the pastry lid on top of the pudding. Wet the outer edge of the lid with a little water, then fold the overhanging pastry over from the sides onto the pie lid and lightly press it down.

Cut two circles of parchment paper and a circle of aluminium foil twice the diameter of the top of the basin. Place both layers of parchment paper on top of the foil and butter the top sheet of parchment paper. Make one 2cm wide pleat directly across the middle of the circle and then lay them, buttered side down, across the top of the pudding basin. Using a length of string, secure the paper and foil firmly around the neck of the basin, then make one tie of string across the top to act as a handle for lifting the basin in and out of the pan during cooking. Make sure the string is tightly tied and secure as you don't want it to break while lifting.

Take a pan with a lid that is large enough to hold the basin with a little space around the sides. Fill the pan with enough water to reach halfway up the sides of the basin. Bring the water up to a boil and then carefully lower in the basin, making sure that the water does not touch the paper and foil lid and put the lid on the pan. Lower the heat to a simmer and gently steam the pudding for 2 hours. Do not remove the lid from the pan during the first 30 minutes of cooking as the drop in temperature may cause the pudding to collapse. After at least 30 minutes, check the water level in the pan at regular intervals and, if necessary, top up with boiling water from the kettle, taking care not to pour water onto the foil and paper lid.

Using a damp dish towel, lift the basin out of the pan. Carefully remove the parchment paper and foil lid. Sit the basin on the damp dish towel and place a large deep-lipped plate inverted over the top. With one hand pressed firmly on the base of the plate and gripping the damp dish towel with your other hand, quickly flip over the basin so that the pudding now sits on the plate. Remove the basin and serve the pudding immediately with some braised red cabbage.

Full English Pie

This pie is an absolute treat to enjoy on a lazy Sunday morning. There isn't a huge amount of work that goes into this pie, so you can prep it the night before, wake up a little earlier than everyone in the morning and just pop it straight in the oven; the smell of the pie will get them out of their beds. Put the coffee on, lay the newspapers out and have brown sauce at the ready for the Full English Pie.

SERVES 6

Line a large baking tray with baking parchment. On a lightly floured surface, roll out 600g of the pastry dough into a large rectangle 1cm thick. Place the rolled-out pastry on the lined tray and chill in the refrigerator for 30 minutes or in the freezer for 15 minutes.

Roll out the remaining pastry dough into a rectangle 1cm thick and lay a sheet of baking parchment on top then set aside in the refrigerator.

Lightly grease the inside of the loaf tin with the butter. Cut a long, thin strip of baking parchment the same width as the base of the tin, then lay it inside the tin so that the base and ends are covered and any excess parchment hangs well over each end. Remove the large rectangle of rolled-out dough from the refrigerator and place it back on the floured surface. Sit the loaf tin in the middle of the pastry. Using a sharp knife, cut diagonal lines from each corner of the tin to the nearest corner of the pastry. Next, carefully line the tin with the pastry, pressing the pastry against the sides of the tin and the overlapping seams firmly back together (see page 28). Trim any overhanging pastry around the top edges of the tin back to 2cm. Put the pastry-lined tin back in the refrigerator to chill for 30 minutes.

Meanwhile, bring a pan of water to the boil and fill a large bowl with iced water and keep it close by. Carefully lower the eggs into the boiling water with a spoon, making sure you don't crack them on the base of the pan, and boil for 6 minutes. Using a slotted spoon, remove the eggs from the pan and transfer to the bowl of iced water. Leave the eggs to cool for 10 minutes. If necessary, add more ice after 5 minutes to keep the water very cold. Once cool enough to handle, peel the shells from the eggs and set aside on paper towels in the refrigerator.

Heat the vegetable oil in a large frying pan over a high heat for 1 minute. Add the mushrooms to the pan and sauté for 3-4 minutes until starting to colour. Transfer to a plate, sprinkle with a pinch of salt and set aside to cool.

800g shortcrust pastry (see page 56 or shop-bought)
10g plain flour, for dusting
5g butter, for greasing
1 egg yolk beaten with 1 teaspoon water, for brushing

For the filling
6 medium eggs
1 tablespoon vegetable oil
200g chestnut mushrooms, cleaned and quartered
800g Cumberland sausages, skins removed
120g black pudding, cut into 1cm dice
150g streaky bacon rashers, cut widthways into 1cm strips
60g sundried tomatoes, drained and roughly chopped
10g fine table salt
freshly ground black pepper

Equipment
900g (2lb) non-stick loaf tin

...continued on page 161

In a mixing bowl, combine the sausagemeat, black pudding, bacon, sundried tomatoes, sautéed mushrooms, salt and a good few twists of freshly ground black pepper. Using your hands, work everything together well. Weigh the filling mixture and divide it into two equal halves. Remove the pastry-lined tin from the refrigerator and stuff it with one half of the filling mixture, packing it down. Using the back of a dessert spoon, make a small trench down the centre of the filling for the eggs to nestle in.

Using a sharp knife, carefully trim a sliver of white from the top and bottom of each boiled egg (being careful not to slice into the yolk). Neatly line up the eggs along the trench in the filling. Depending on the length of the loaf tin, you might fit 5 or 6 eggs in the channel. Cover the eggs with the remaining filling mixture, making sure it goes down the sides, gently packing it down and lightly flattening the surface.

Remove the smaller rectangle of pastry from the refrigerator and with a diamond shaped cutter, cut out a lattice shape (see page 33 for photograph).

Wet the overhanging pastry with a little water and then lay the rectangle of pastry across the top of the pie. Firmly crimp together the overhanging pastry edges and the pie lid (see page 32). Brush the top of the pie with the egg wash. Using a skewer, make a couple of small steam holes along the centre of the lid. Put the pie in the refrigerator to chill for 20 minutes.

Preheat the oven to 200°C fan/220°C/gas mark 7.

When ready to bake, lightly brush the pie with egg wash for one final time. Place the tin in the preheated oven and bake the pie for 1 hour or until the pastry is golden brown and the core temperature of the filling has reached 50°C on a digital probe thermometer. Remove from the oven and allow the pie to rest in the tin for 15 minutes.

Carefully lift the pie out of the tin by pulling on both ends of the strip of baking parchment. Slice the pie and serve while hot.

Beef, Stilton & Onion Pie

This is a pie for wintry days when the roads are blocked and you are snowed in.
It is rich, decadent and best followed by a nap on the couch.

SERVES 4–6

300g rough puff pastry (see
    page 66, or shop-bought
    puff pastry)
1 egg yolk beaten with
    1 teaspoon water,
    for brushing

For the filling
600g beef chuck steak, cut
    into 4cm dice
100g plain flour
40ml vegetable oil
4 Spanish onions, peeled
    and halved but with the
    roots left on
400g chestnut mushrooms,
    halved
1 teaspoon table salt
300ml red wine
2 bay leaves
3 thyme sprigs
2 litres beef stock
100g Stilton cheese, broken
    into 2cm nuggets
½ teaspoon freshly ground
    black pepper

Equipment
pie dish (25cm long and
    5cm deep)

Preheat the oven to 220°C fan/240°C/gas mark 9.

To prepare the filling, put the beef in a roasting tray, dust with the flour and toss the beef until all the flour has been absorbed by the meat. Add 20ml of the vegetable oil to the tray and toss well to make sure the meat is evenly coated. Put the tray in to the preheated oven and roast the beef for 20 minutes until browned and any juices released during cooking have evaporated.

While the beef is roasting, cut each onion half into six wedges through the root to leave petals. Put a large frying pan over a medium heat, add the remaining 20ml of vegetable oil and warm for 1 minute. Add the onions to the pan and cook, stirring frequently with a wooden spoon until the onions have started to brown. Add the mushrooms to the pan with half the salt and continue to cook for a further 3 minutes until the mushrooms have just softened. Next, add the red wine, bay leaves and thyme and bring to a simmer.

After 20 minutes, remove the beef from the oven and check it is nicely browned. If not, return it to the oven for a further 5 minutes. When the beef is ready, tip the onions, mushrooms, herbs and red wine into the roasting tray over the top of the meat. Put the frying pan back on the heat and pour in the beef stock – half at a time, if necessary – and bring to a simmer. Add to the tray with all the other pie filling ingredients.

At this stage, take the time to make sure the beef is not stuck to the bottom of the roasting tray: using a wooden spoon, dislodge any caramelised chunks of meat. Working carefully as the tray is hot, tightly cover the top of the tray with aluminium foil. Return the tray to the oven and continue to cook at 220°C fan/240°C/gas mark 9 for 10 minutes, then reduce the temperature to 160°C fan/180°C/gas mark 4 and set a timer for 1¾ hours.

…continued on page 166

While the filling is braising, prepare the pastry. Line a baking tray with parchment paper. On a lightly floured surface, roll out the pastry to a 5mm thick circle large enough to cover the pie dish. Slide the rolled-out pastry onto the lined tray and chill in the refrigerator for at least 25 minutes. Set aside any pastry trimmings for decoration.

After the beef has been braising for 1¾ hours, remove the tray from the oven and, using a dish towel to protect your hands, carefully peel back a corner of the foil. Spoon out one chunk of beef and check to make sure it is tender. It is okay if the beef has a little bite left in it, but it should not be chewy. If necessary, pop the tray back in the oven for a further 15 minutes and check again.

When the beef is ready, carefully remove all the foil from the roasting tray. Place a colander over a large bowl and tip in the filling. Let the mixture strain for a couple of minutes, then place the contents of the colander back into the tray and spread around to cool down. Transfer the strained liquid from the bowl to a large saucepan, bring to a simmer over a medium heat and cook until thick enough to coat the back of a spoon. Season with the pepper and the remaining salt, adding a little at a time, stirring and tasting until it has the correct level of seasoning. Pour the reduced liquid over the mixture in the tray and set aside to cool to room temperature, stirring occasionally to speed up the process. Once the mixture is cool, transfer the filling to the pie dish and level the surface. Nudge the nuggets of Stilton into the filling, distributing them evenly across the surface but avoiding the sides.

Increase the oven temperature to 200°C fan/220°C/gas mark 7.

Brush the rim of the pie dish with the egg wash, brushing about 2.5cm down the sides of the dish. Lay the pastry circle centrally across the top of the dish, allowing it to rest lightly on top of the filling. (The pastry lid should not be taut as it may droop during cooking and tear.) Press firmly down on the pastry against the egg-brushed rim of the dish to seal all the way round. Lightly brush the pie lid with more egg wash and decorate however you prefer using the reserved pastry trimming (see page 33) and then brush that with egg wash. Return the pie to the refrigerator and chill for a further 20 minutes.

Place the dish on a rack in the centre of the preheated oven and bake the pie for 25 minutes or until the pastry is golden brown and the core temperature of the filling has reached at least 70°C on a digital probe thermometer. Alternatively, poke the tip of a knife through the pie into the middle of the filling and leave it there for a few seconds – it should be hot to the touch. Halfway through the cooking time, turn the dish around in the oven to ensure an even bake.

Serve the pie simply with some boiled new potatoes and slow-roasted carrots.

Lamb Hotpot

If you get this dish on the go mid-Sunday morning, the house will smell of delicious roasted lamb by the afternoon; a perfect way to build anticipation!

SERVES 6

Preheat the oven to 200°C fan/220°C/gas mark 7. Rub the lamb with the oil and season well with sea salt. Place the lamb on a wire rack set over a roasting tray. Place the tray in the preheated oven and roast the lamb for 25 minutes.

Remove the tray from the oven and carefully lift the wire rack with the lamb out of the tray. Reduce the oven temperature to 170°C fan/190°C/gas mark 5. Pour any lamb fat that has collected in the tray into a small bowl and set aside. Pour 250ml of water into the tray, place the lamb inside and tightly cover the top of the tray with aluminium foil. Return the tray to the oven and roast for 2½ hours. After the lamb has been roasting for 2½ hours, remove the tray from the oven and, using a dish towel to protect your hands from the hot steam, carefully peel back the foil. Transfer the lamb to a chopping board to rest and pour any juices from the roasting tray into a bowl and set aside.

Warm a large, deep casserole dish with a lid over a medium heat and add 2 tablespoons of the reserved lamb fat. When the fat is bubbling, add the carrots and cook for 5 minutes until caramelised, stirring occasionally. Add the onions to the casserole and cook for 4 minutes, then lower the heat to low–medium and cook until lightly browned. Next, add the celery and cook for a further 2 minutes. Dust the vegetables with the flour and, stirring with a wooden spoon, cook for 4 minutes. Add the reserved lamb juices, stock, Worcestershire sauce, rosemary, bay leaves, plenty of freshly ground black pepper and the table salt. Increase the heat to low–medium and bring everything to a simmer, reducing the stock until it coats the back of a spoon.

Slice the lamb into chunks, discarding the bones and any excess fat. Add the meat to the casserole and remove from the heat.

To make the potato topping, put the potato slices in a colander and season with the salt, tossing well to ensure all the slices are coated. Leave to sit for 5 minutes then rinse the potato slices in cold water and dab them dry with a clean dish towel. Starting in the middle of the casserole, arrange the potato slices in neat concentric circles working right to the outside of the dish. Put the lid on the casserole and put the dish back in the oven to cook for 1 hour. After 1 hour, remove the lid from the casserole and brush the potato slices with the melted butter. Increase the oven temperature to 190°C fan/210°C/gas mark 6½. Return the dish to the oven without the lid and cook the hotpot for a further 20 minutes. Remove from the oven and leave to cool for 10 minutes before serving.

2–2.5kg shoulder of lamb
1 tablespoon vegetable oil
4 carrots, peeled and roughly cut into chunks
3 Spanish onions, peeled and roughly chopped
3 celery stalks, roughly cut into chunks
20g plain flour
500ml lamb stock
2 teaspoons Worcestershire sauce
20g rosemary, leaves picked and finely chopped
2 bay leaves
1 teaspoon table salt
sea salt and freshly ground black pepper, to taste

For the potato topping
1kg King Edward or Desiree potatoes, peeled and cut into 3mm-thick slices
2 teaspoons salt
20g butter, melted

Keema-Spiced Cottage Pie

This is a quick-to-make mix-up of British and Indian classics in a single dish.
It is light enough to eat as a summer supper and an absolute family favourite at
the Franklins.

──────────────── SERVES 4 ────────────────

Preheat the oven to 180°C fan/200°C/gas mark 6.

Heat the oil in a large frying pan over a medium heat. Add the onion and sauté for
10 minutes until it starts to brown. Add the turmeric, garam masala and cumin
seeds and toast for 2 minutes. Add the garlic, ginger and chilli, then sauté for a
further 5 minutes until soft and lightly browned. Add the beef mince and sauté
until any liquid has evaporated and then add the tomatoes and cook for a further
15 minutes. Add the peas and coriander leaves. Taste and adjust the seasoning,
if necessary, then spoon into a 24cm round ovenproof pie dish, level the surface
and allow to cool.

For the potato topping, boil the potatoes in a pan of salted water for 15–20
minutes or until soft in the centre and then drain. Add the milk, butter and
turmeric, then mash together well. Finally, fold in the egg yolk and mix well
to combine.

Spread the potato topping over the minced beef mixture in the pie dish. Ruffle
the surface of the potato topping with a fork for added texture.

Place the dish in the preheated oven and bake the pie for 30 minutes or until the
beef mixture is bubbling up the sides of the dish and the potato topping has a
crispy golden crust. Serve immediately.

1 tablespoon vegetable oil
1 medium onion, finely diced
½ teaspoon ground turmeric
2 teaspoons garam masala
½ teaspoon cumin seeds
2 garlic cloves, minced
2 teaspoons grated fresh
    root ginger
2 red chillies, finely chopped
500g beef mince
350g tinned chopped tomatoes
300g frozen peas, defrosted
25g coriander, leaves picked

For the potato topping
1kg peeled potatoes, cut
    into chunks
150ml milk
80g unsalted butter
1 teaspoon ground turmeric
1 egg yolk

Equipment
24cm round ovenproof pie dish

Venison & Bone Marrow Suet Pie

A dish for a dark, cold winter night, this is a showpiece for the centre of the family table. The marrow bones not only look spectacular protruding from the crispy suet pastry crust but the marrow melts into the pie itself, adding luxury.

We count ourselves lucky to have wild venison available at the Holborn Dining Room to use in cooking, it's a delicious meat and highly sustainable. My friend Mike Robinson took our team out recently to stalk deer in the Cotswolds, and the trip was hugely important in teaching us to respect the ingredients we use and how Mike manages the land he hunts on so that everything remains sustainable, removing a little of the supply chain that so often cuts chefs off from mental responsibility. It was probably the most educational trip we have ever been on. When you have to physically carry the animal from the forest, you then cook it with extra care and attention.

Venison as a wild meat is naturally lean so it's important to follow the braising instructions and not cook it for hours and hours as it will dry out. Enjoy the suet crust, it's a different beast when roasted instead of steamed and I adore it on a slow-cooked meat pie.

— SERVES 6 —

300g suet pastry (see page 70)
1 egg yolk beaten with
    1 teaspoon water,
    for brushing

For the filling
1kg venison stewing steak, cut
    into 3cm dice
60g plain flour
30ml vegetable oil
4 onions, peeled and sliced
300ml red wine
1.5 litres beef stock
¼ bunch of thyme, leaves
    picked, plus extra to sprinkle
25g table salt
3 large carrots, peeled and cut
    into 1cm chunks
3 x 10–12cm centre-cut marrow
    bones, soaked in cold water
    overnight
½ teaspoon sea salt

Preheat the oven to 220°C fan/240°C/gas mark 9.

To make the filling, place the venison in a large roasting tray, coat in the flour and then rub all over with 20ml of the vegetable oil. Place the tray in the preheated oven and roast the venison for 20 minutes or until it is well browned and any liquid has evaporated.

Lower the oven temperature to 180°C fan/200°C/gas mark 6.

Meanwhile, heat the remaining vegetable oil in a cast-iron pan. Add the onions and sweat them down until softened and lightly browned.

Remove the tray from the oven and deglaze with the red wine, scraping up any crusty bits that have stuck to the bottom. Add the venison and the red wine juices from the tray to the pan with the onions. Add the beef stock, thyme and salt and then bring up to a simmer. Cover the pan with foil and put it in the oven to braise the meat for 1½ hours.

After 1½ hours, check the venison is not sticking to the bottom of the pan and add the carrots. Continue to cook for a further 30 minutes or until the venison is tender.

Strain the liquid from the meat into a second pan and reduce over a medium heat until it has the consistency of gravy. Return the reduction to the first pan and fold it back through the venison mixture. Spread out the filling mixture in a large ovenproof pie dish and leave to cool to room temperature. When the filling mixture has cooled, place the three marrow bones in the pie dish, spacing them evenly apart from each other and the sides of the dish.

Roll the pastry out into a circle that is 5cm wider in diameter than the rim of the pie dish. Lightly brush the rim of the dish with some of the egg wash, which will act as a glue to seal the pastry lid to the pie dish.

Cut three small crosses into the pastry lid where the marrow bones will poke through. Lay the pastry lid on top of the pie and wiggle the bones through the cross-shaped cuts. Firmly press the pastry lid against the egg-washed rim of the pie dish and squeeze the pastry around the bottom of the marrow bones to seal.

Lightly brush the pastry lid all over with the egg wash, sprinkle with sea salt a few thyme leaves, then place in the refrigerator for 15 minutes to chill.

Increase the oven temperature to 190°C fan/210°C/gas mark 6½.

Place the pie dish on a rack in the centre of the preheated oven and bake the pie for 40 minutes or until the pastry is golden brown. Halfway through the cooking time, turn the dish around in the oven to ensure an even bake.

Serve immediately while warm with hasselback potatoes alongside.

Equipment
large ovenproof pie dish

Rabbit, Pancetta & Mustard Pie

The three main ingredients in this pie are destined to be together. In the restaurant we sometimes serve a braised rabbit leg with mashed potato and the same sauce – it sells like hot cakes. Ask your butcher to break down the rabbits as mentioned below or, if you are confident, prepare it yourself. But I would probably ask my butcher to do it anyway as he loves prepping rabbits.

SERVES 6

700g rough puff pastry (see page 66, or shop-bought puff pastry)

5g butter

1 egg yolk beaten with 1 teaspoon water, for brushing

Minted Bean Salad (see page 240)

For the filling

2 rabbits, legs and shoulders removed but left on the bone, loins removed and cut into 1.5cm dice, carcass chopped in half and head discarded

1 hispi cabbage, heart removed and finely shredded

100ml white wine

2 teaspoons vegetable oil

40g butter

2 Spanish onions, peeled and sliced

200g pancetta, diced

40g plain flour

1 tablespoon wholegrain mustard

1 tablespoon Dijon mustard

4 thyme sprigs, leaves picked

1 teaspoon table salt

Equipment

23cm round non-stick, springform cake tin

Line a large baking tray with parchment paper. On a lightly floured surface, roll one-third of the pastry out to a 5mm thick circle. Slide the rolled-out pastry onto the lined baking tray and chill in the refrigerator until needed.

Grease a 23cm round springform cake tin with the butter. Roll out the remaining two-thirds of the pastry to a 5mm thick circle. Line the greased tin with the rolled-out pastry, firmly pressing it into the base and sides. Leaving 3cm overhanging all the way round, trim the excess pastry around the edge of the tin, reserving the trimmings for decorating. Place the pastry-lined tin in refrigerator to chill while you make the pie filling.

To make the filling, put the rabbit legs, shoulders and carcass in a large pan and cover with 2 litres of water. Bring the water to a simmer, skimming off any scum that rises to the surface, and cook for 1½ hours until the meat is just tender. Using a slotted spoon, remove the rabbit carcass from the pan and discard. Add the shredded cabbage to the pan and cook for 1 minute. Strain the stock through a colander into a second pan, setting aside the meat and cabbage to cool. Add the white wine to the stock in the pan, bring to the boil over a high heat and reduce by two-thirds. Transfer the reduced stock to a jug and set aside.

Warm the vegetable oil and butter in a pan over a medium heat until bubbling. Add the onions and pancetta and cook for 6 minutes until just softened. Stir in the flour and cook over a low heat for a further 5 minutes. Meanwhile, pick the meat off the shoulders and legs, discarding any bones.

Add half the reduced stock to the onion and pancetta mixture and bring up to a simmer. Allow the sauce to thicken, then add the rest of the stock and repeat.

...continued on page 178

Increase the heat and bring the sauce to the boil. Stirring continuously, allow the sauce to reduce for 2 minutes. Add the mustard, thyme and salt and stir again. Squeeze any excess moisture out of the cabbage and add to the pan along with the rabbit meat. Spread out the mix in a wide dish or tray and leave to cool to room temperature before putting it in the refrigerator to chill for 20 minutes.

Remove the pastry-lined tin from the refrigerator. Spoon the chilled pie filling into the pastry case and level the surface. Lightly brush the overhanging edges of the pastry case with the egg wash. Lay the pastry lid on top of the pie and lightly brush with the egg wash. Firmly join the edges and crimp over onto the lid by at least 3cm (see page 32) so the pie is sealed all the way round. Lightly brush again with the egg wash, this time brushing the crimped edges too, and decorate however you prefer using the reserved pastry trimmings (see page 33). Return the pie to the refrigerator and chill for 20 minutes.

Preheat the oven to 190°C fan/210°C/gas mark 6½.

Place the tin on a shelf in the centre of the preheated oven and bake the pie for 45 minutes or until the pastry is golden brown. Halfway through the cooking time, turn the tin around in the oven to ensure an even bake.

To serve, pop the pie out of the springform tin. Cut into wedges and serve alongside my minted bean salad.

Light Game Pie

It is tempting to veer towards hearty, red wine-based dishes when devising game recipes, but at the very start of the hunting season I prefer to cook in a much lighter fashion. A less heavy style of cooking is kinder to the more gently flavoured game birds, such as pheasant and guinea fowl. This pie is also a softer introduction to game if you find offal-rich dishes a little intimidating.

SERVES 4–6

Grease a 23cm round non-stick, springform cake tin with butter and line a baking tray with parchment paper. On a lightly floured surface, roll out one-third of the pastry to a 5mm thick circle that is 1cm wider than the tin. Slide the rolled-out pastry onto the lined tray and chill in the refrigerator until needed. Roll out the remaining pastry and use it to line the greased tin (see page 26), reserving any pastry trimmings for decoration. Place the pastry-lined tin in the refrigerator while you make the filling.

First, prepare the pheasants and guinea fowl. Remove the breasts from the birds, skin them and slice into 3cm dice. Remove the legs but leave them on the bone. Discard the carcasses.

Pour the chicken stock into a saucepan and add the carrots, onions, garlic and salt. Bring to the boil over a high heat, drop in the prepared legs, reduce the heat to low and simmer for 45 minutes. Using tongs, remove the legs from the pan and set aside on a plate to cool.

Drop the diced breast meat into the hot stock, turn the heat off and leave to poach for 5 minutes. Using a slotted spoon, remove the meat, carrots, onions and garlic from the stock and transfer to a large mixing bowl and leave to cool.

Pass the stock through a strainer or fine-mesh sieve into a clean pan. Place the pan over a medium heat and, using a spoon, skim any excess fat from the surface of the stock every 10 minutes until it has reduced to about 200ml.

Strip the skin off the cooked legs, then flake the meat into large pieces, making sure you remove all bones. Add the flaked leg meat to the bowl. Now, trim any roots off the onions, separate them into petals and add to the bowl.

...continued on page 181

700g rough puff pastry (see page 66, or shop-bought puff pastry)
10g butter, for greasing
1 egg yolk beaten with 1 teaspoon water, for brushing

For the filling
2 pheasants
1 guinea fowl
1.5 litres chicken stock
3 large carrots, peeled and roughly chopped
2 large onions, peeled and quartered, but with root still attached
2 garlic cloves, peeled and crushed
1 teaspoon sea salt
140g unsalted butter
150g plain flour
330ml dry cider
1 teaspoon English mustard
1 teaspoon wholegrain mustard
10g flat-leaf parsley, roughly chopped

Equipment
23cm round non-stick, springform cake tin

Melt the butter in a saucepan over a low heat. When the butter has melted, add the flour and, whisking continuously, cook for 10 minutes to make a roux. Add half the cider to the pan and whisk again until the sauce is smooth. Add the remaining cider while continuing to whisk the sauce. The sauce will be quite thick at this stage, but that helps to keep it smooth. Next, add half the stock and whisk again, before adding the remaining stock. If the sauce looks a little thin, increase the heat slightly and cook while whisking continuously until it is thick enough to coat the back of a spoon. Add the mustards and flat-leaf parsley, then taste and, if necessary, add more seasoning.

Pour the sauce over the cooked meat and vegetables in the bowl, then stir to combine well. Leave the mixture to cool to room temperature, then place the bowl in the refrigerator and chill for 20 minutes or until completely cold.

Remove the pastry-lined tin and rolled-out pastry lid from the refrigerator. Spoon the chilled pie filling into the pastry case and level the surface. Lightly brush the overhanging edges of the pastry case with the egg wash. Lay the pastry lid on top of the pie and lightly brush with the egg wash. When the overhanging lip of the pastry case is pliable enough, firmly join the edges and crimp over onto the lid by at least 3cm (see page 32) so the pie is sealed all the way round. Lightly brush again with the egg wash, this time brushing the crimped edges too, and decorate however you prefer using the reserved pastry trimmings (see page 33). Return the pie to the refrigerator and chill for 20 minutes.

Preheat the oven to 200°C fan/220°C/gas mark 7.

Place the tin on a shelf in the centre of the preheated oven and bake the pie for 45 minutes or until the pastry is golden brown and the core temperature of the filling has reached at least 65°C on a digital probe thermometer. Halfway through the cooking time, turn the tin around in the oven to ensure an even bake.

To serve, pop the pie out of the springform tin and slice. As this pie is pretty much a complete meal in itself, I tend to serve it on its own, but if you can't go without potatoes then you can always have some mash alongside.

GRAND PARTY
PIECES

Stuffed Sea Bass en Croute

Sometimes there are moments at work where I stop and giggle at what I actually do for a living, whether it's running around a toyshop looking for parts to make a mechanical pie that has been commissioned or hiding away in a room in the British Library looking at ancient recipes. Don't get me wrong, this job can be incredibly tough at times, but I do feel lucky to be doing what I love.

I have very fond memories of making this dish in Las Vegas for a collaboration dinner we were invited to cook at by chef Joshua Smith from Bardot Brasserie. Josh is my type of chef, cooking classically with great ingredients with a clear honesty in his food. He is also a complete dude and he and his amazing wife Signe remain friends to this day. For the dinner he wanted a night of pure classics, with crafted dishes steeped in history, so we had an antique duck press at the table at one point and the most incredible, theatrical desserts from the pastry team. There was a point early in the day of the event where six of us were all making the pastry scales together for the sea bass en croute. It was a moment of joy in a hard, busy week, all of us kind of looking at each other thinking, 'we actually get paid to make giant pastry fish'. This is a slightly simpler version of the sea bass en croute served that night, but just as joyous to make and no less tasty.

SERVES 6

2 large whole sea bass fillets,
   minimum 500g each,
   pin-boned and scaled
1 teaspoon table salt
10 slices (150g)
   prosciutto crudo
600g classic puff pastry (see
   page 63, or shop-bought)
2 egg yolks beaten with 2
   teaspoons water,
   for brushing
White Butter Sauce (see
   page 255), to serve

For the stuffing
100g pitted green olives,
   finely chopped
100g gherkins, finely diced
30g capers, finely chopped
30g flat-leaf parsley,
   leaves picked
zest of 1 lemon

To make the stuffing, combine the olives, gherkins, capers, parsley and lemon zest in a bowl. Lay the two sea bass fillets skin side down and season with the salt. Spread the stuffing mixture over one fillet and then sandwich the other on top with the skin side facing up.

Tear off a sheet of clingfilm large enough to wrap the fish. Lay the prosciutto slices on the clingfilm, slightly overlapping one another, to make a rectangle. Place the stuffed fish along the bottom edge of the rectangle and then roll to wrap it in the prosciutto slices. The fish should be completely sealed within the prosciutto. Tightly wrap the whole thing in clingfilm and chill in the refrigerator for 20 minutes.

Line a large baking tray with parchment paper. On a lightly floured surface, roll out one-third of the pastry to a 5mm thick oval (with a tail, if you like, large enough for the fish to fit with at least a 5cm border around the outside. Remove the fish from the refrigerator and unwrap the clingfilm. Place the fish in the middle of the pastry and brush the area that is exposed around it with egg wash.

...continued on page 186

Roll out the remaining pastry again to a 5mm thick oval, but this time one-quarter bigger than the previous shape. Lay the pastry over the top of the fish, smooth it down with your hands to make sure there are no air pockets and then seal it down to the pastry base. Slide the pastry parcel onto the lined baking tray and chill in the refrigerator for 10 minutes to firm up a little.

Remove the tray from the refrigerator and, using a fork, work around the edges of the pastry base, pressing firmly to leave the imprint of the tines. If necessary, dust the fork with a little flour to stop it sticking. Trim the edges of the pastry to accentuate the fish's shape and then lightly brush with egg wash all over. Rest in the refrigerator for 30 minutes.

Preheat the oven to 200°C fan/220°C/gas mark 8.

Using a small sharp knife, score scale shapes down the length of the pastry, being careful not to cut right through the dough. Brush the pastry again with more of the egg wash. Place the tray in the preheated oven and bake the fish for 25 minutes, until the pastry is golden brown. Serve immediately with the butter sauce.

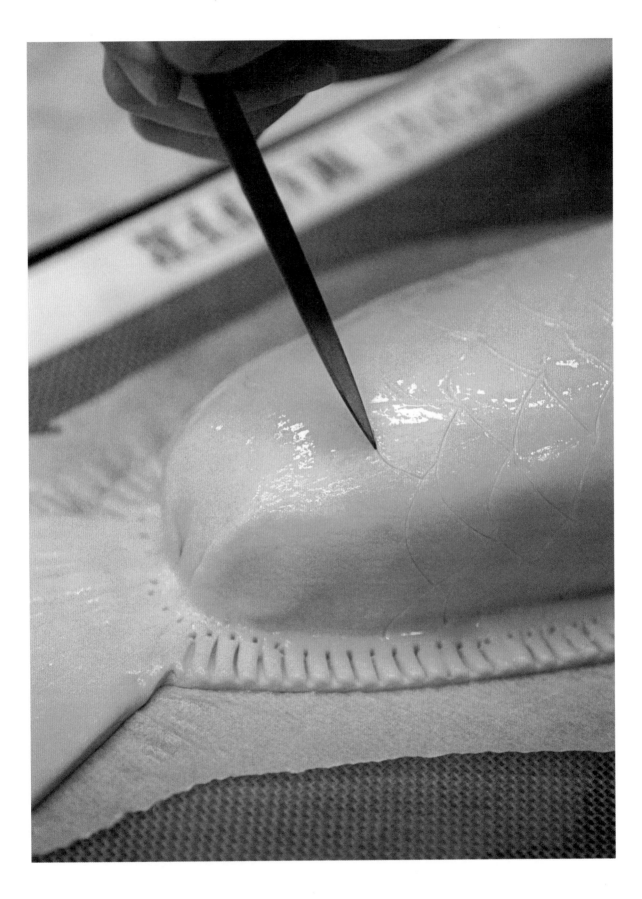

Honey & Five-Spiced Glazed Ham

When done properly, a glistening, mahogany-coloured, honey-glazed roast ham
in the middle of a dining table is jaw-dropping. As it feeds so many, a ham is
great for any large family gathering, where people can come and take a slice off
whenever they feel like it. Plus there is the benefit of leftovers the next day too. It
is important to use a pan big enough to cook the whole ham, as it will need to be
submerged in water throughout the entire cooking process – so beg, borrow or
steal a giant pan if you don't already have one.

SERVES 12

Put the gammon joint in a large pan and cover the meat completely with cold
water. Bring to a simmer over a low-medium heat; skim off and discard any scum
that rises to the surface of the water until it has mostly stopped. If necessary,
top up the pan with more water. Add the celery, carrots, onion, leek, garlic and
bay leaves and bring back up to a simmer.

Gently simmer the gammon for 2½ hours, topping up with more water as
necessary so the meat is always covered. If your pan is not quite large enough to
cover the meat completely, turn the gammon over halfway through the cooking
time. If your gammon joint weighs less than 5kg, simmer for 20 minutes per
500g.

Insert a digital probe thermometer into the centre of the gammon joint. It needs
to read 70°C or above. If necessary, continue to cook the meat until it reaches
the required temperature.

Preheat the oven to 190°C fan/210°C/gas mark 7.

Wrap a clean dish towel around the largest exposed bone at the top of the
gammon joint, and carefully pull the meat out of the pan and place it in a
roasting tray on a chopping board. Set aside the cooking liquid to use later
for the glaze.

Using a small, thin knife, carefully strip the rind from the outside of the gammon
joint, leaving the layer of fat underneath intact as much as possible (this will
protect the meat and stop it drying out). Let the rind fall into the tray. Without
slicing into the meat, score the fat in a decorative diamond pattern: take the
knife from one corner to the other, scoring parallel lines 2cm apart, then repeat
in the opposite direction. Push a single clove into the centre of each 'X' or the
corner of each diamond shape. Remove all the rind from the tray and discard.

5kg bone-in, unsmoked
    gammon joint
2 celery stalks,
    roughly chopped
2 carrots, peeled and
    roughly chopped
1 onion, peeled and halved
1 leek, roughly chopped
3 garlic cloves
4 bay leaves
40 cloves
150ml runny honey
1 teaspoon five-spice powder

Equipment
digital probe thermometer

...continued on page 192

Place the tray in the preheated oven and roast the gammon joint for 10 minutes. After the first 10 minutes, turn the tray in the oven and cook for a further 10 minutes.

Pour 2 medium ladlefuls of the reserved cooking liquid into the roasting tray. (The remaining cooking liquid can either be discarded or used as a stock for soup, however, it will be quite salty so be careful with seasoning.) Add the honey and five-spice powder to the tray and mix with the cooking juices in the bottom of the tray to make the glaze. Baste the meat all over with the glaze, pushing it into the scored lines with a brush, and then return to the oven for a further 10 minutes. Continue to baste the gammon joint every 5 minutes, turning the meat in the tray each time until it is covered in a sticky glaze.

Carefully remove the glazed ham from the oven. Place on a large platter and then slice and serve.

Pork Belly & Apple Sauce

This is the best method for cooking crispy skinned pork belly with tender, melting meat inside. Roasting at a very low temperature for a prolonged amount of time means that the fat breaks down but does not disappear, which is often the problem with pork belly when it has been overcooked. I have borrowed the wok method from Chinese cooking to create the most incredible crackling. If you want to avoid using a wok, take the pork out of the oven after the slow cook, turn the oven temperature right up to 260°C, rub the belly with a little oil and then roast it for 15–20 minutes. Although the resulting crackling is still good, it will not be quite as good as the wok method and it will definitely be a little smoky in your kitchen.

SERVES 8-10

half a long pork belly (2–2.5kg),
  ribs and cartilage removed,
  skin left on
2 garlic cloves, peeled and
  finely chopped
30g sage, leaves picked and
  finely chopped
25g table salt
200ml vegetable oil

For the apple sauce
500g Bramley apples, peeled,
  cored and sliced
½ lemon
20g caster sugar

To serve
Clapshot (see page 232)
Slow-Roasted Carrots
  & Cumin (see page 242)

Equipment
wok (optional)

Preheat the oven to 90°C fan/110°C/gas mark ¼.

Using a very sharp knife or Stanley knife, score the pork belly through the skin with diagonal cuts 2.5cm apart. Turn the belly over and rub in the garlic, sage and 20g of the salt. Trim a little fat off the bottom edge on a slant, then roll the pork tightly into the centre to form a cigar shape.

Tie one loop of butchers string tightly around the middle of the belly to hold it in place and then tie at each end. Finally tie tight loops in between these. Tying the middle and ends first will keep the belly evenly rolled.

Put the rolled pork belly in a clean sink. Boil a full kettle of water and, as soon as it boils, pour the water all over the skin. Repeat once more. Dab the skin dry with a clean dish towel. Put the pork in a roasting tray and rub in the remaining salt. Place the tray in the preheated oven and roast the pork for 6 hours.

Take a large wok and set a small rack over the top that will hold the pork belly but also leaves a small gap for a ladle. Pour the vegetable oil into the wok and heat to 180°C or until the surface of the oil is shimmering. Ladle the oil continuously over the skin of the pork belly until it no longer bubbles and is fully crispy. Leave the meat to rest for 15 minutes.

Meanwhile, make the apple sauce. Put the apples into a plastic bowl with the lemon juice and sugar. Cover the bowl tightly with clingfilm and cook in a microwave on full power for 4 minutes. (Alternatively, cook the apples in a saucepan with the lemon juice and sugar over a low heat for 10–15 minutes or until the fruit has roughly broken down.) Carefully peel back the clingfilm and mash up the apple with a fork. Carve the pork into thick slices and serve with the apple sauce, clapshot and slow-roasted carrots.

The Ultimate Beef Wellington

From the first moment we started discussing this book, one of the key things I always wanted to include was a comprehensive guide to making a restaurant-quality beef wellington at home. This is not the exact method we use to make beef wellington in The Pie Room kitchen – that just is not practical – but rather how best to replicate it in your home kitchen. Working in different professional kitchens over the past 20 years, I've made wellingtons under different chefs, but for the last five years I've been serving mine. Even over those five years, my method has evolved – and this is it.

A beef wellington of real quality, one that blows away your dinner guests, takes time and discipline. If you follow the steps below properly, you will have a wellington to be really proud of at the end. Below is a list of the most important factors to consider when making a wellington:

1. Allow yourself plenty of time. Do not attempt to make a wellington when you get home from work to serve for dinner that evening, it will not turn out well. I have split the work involved over two days, so if you want to do this as a weekend project, prepare the meat and mushroom duxelles on a Saturday so you are doing just the pastry work on the Sunday before sitting down to eat. Chilling the meat overnight makes it easier to handle and roll, plus it means everything will be as cold as possible when it goes in the oven, giving the pastry more time to cook.

2. Use the best quality beef you can afford for a superior flavour. Furthermore, dry-aged beef will release less moisture during cooking, helping to protect the pastry from becoming soggy.

3. Plan your timings meticulously. If you have told your guests what time they will be eating, work back from that hour and make sure to factor in enough time for both decorating the wellington and resting the meat on top of the cooking time.

4. REST THE WELLINGTON FOR A MINIMUM OF 30 MINUTES. I cannot stress enough how important this is. If you cut a slice of wellington without resting the meat, the beef will still be under tension from the cooking, the meat fibres will suddenly relax and all the cooking juices will flood out into the wellington, leaving the meat dry and the pastry soggy.

5. Do not use my classic puff pastry from the Doughs chapter with its hundreds of layers – it is too fragile for carving and will create a mess on the table. Instead, use either rough puff pastry (see page 66) or shop-bought puff pastry, which has slightly more strength and structure. Ready-made vegetarian puff pastry, which uses emulsified oils to create the lamination, also works well.

6. Buy a digital probe thermometer. Cooking the beef accurately to a specific temperature gives the best chance of a perfect rosy-pink cut-through.

7. Do not swap bresaola for Parma ham. I have seen this in so many recipes, but Parma ham has too strong a flavour and will only make your wellington taste of pork, which is odd if you think about it. Keep to cured beef and allow the flavour of the fillet to shine through.

8. Follow my guide for cooking times, depending on how you like your beef cooked. At the restaurant I serve beef wellington medium rare, because for me that is when it is at its best, but obviously it's your wellington and so it's your call.

--- SERVES 6-8 ---

DAY ONE

To make the mushroom duxelles, finely chop all the mushrooms to an even size. Take the time to do this by hand as you will achieve a much better texture than by using a food processor, which will always leave uneven chunks. Take a large non-stick pan and warm 20ml of the vegetable oil over a low heat. Add the shallots and garlic to the pan, sweat them down for 10 minutes until soft, then transfer to a bowl and set aside.

Add another 20ml of vegetable oil to the pan and increase the heat to high. Add all the mushrooms and 5g of table salt. The mushrooms will start to release moisture after a few minutes, so cook, stirring, until any moisture has completely evaporated. Add the Madeira and cook until completely reduced, then return the shallots and garlic to the pan with the thyme and rosemary, stir for a minute then remove from the heat and spread across paper towels to remove any more moisture, and cool.

Dry the beef fillet all over with paper towels and then season with table salt. Heat a roasting tray or frying pan large enough to fit the beef fillet with 30ml of vegetable oil over a high heat and then carefully sear the beef all over using tongs. Make sure the oil is hot and shimmering before you add the beef or it will stick to the pan. Never cook for more than 5 seconds on one side – you are looking for an even, lightly caramelised sear, not to cook the beef. Transfer the beef to a plate to cool, then brush all over with the mustard.

Lay a large 50cm x 35cm rectangle of clingfilm on your work surface and then add a second layer. Starting from the middle, flatten out any air bubbles using a clean dish towel. Working from the edge of the clingfilm closest to you, lay out the bresaola slices into a 35cm x 25cm rectangle, slightly overlapping the slices.

...continued on page 200

1kg thick centre-cut beef fillet, trimmed of any sinew
1 teaspoon table salt
30ml vegetable oil
1 tablespoon English mustard
20 slices (around 100g) bresaola
500g large leaf spinach
500g rough puff pastry for the wellington, plus 300g for the lattice (see page 66, or shop-bought puff pastry)
4 egg yolks beaten with 4 teaspoons water, for brushing
½ teaspoon sea salt flakes

For the mushroom duxelles

300g mixed wild mushrooms
400g button mushrooms
300g chestnut mushrooms
40ml vegetable oil
2 banana shallots, peeled and finely chopped
1 garlic clove, peeled and finely chopped
1 teaspoon table salt
100ml Madeira wine
20g thyme, leaves picked
20g rosemary, leaves picked

Equipment

lattice pastry cutter roller (optional) and digital probe thermometer

Dampen a clean dish towel and lay it across a large plate that fits inside your microwave. Spread one-third of the spinach across the section of towel that covers the plate, then cover with the rest of the towel and microwave on full power for 2 minutes. Pull back the towel to expose the spinach and allow to cool for 1 minute. (Alternatively, blanch the spinach leaves in boiling water for 5 seconds, then refresh in iced water.) Carefully peel the spinach off in patches and transfer to a flat dry towel to start building a 30cm x 20cm rectangle. Repeat with the remaining spinach in another two batches until the rectangle is built up. Lay another towel on top and, using a rolling pin, firmly roll across from one end to the other to remove any moisture and fully flatten the spinach.

Carefully lift the dish towel with the spinach by its corners and transfer on top of the bresaola rectangle – you want the spinach to touch the bottom edge of the sliced meat. Peel away the towel. Spread the mushroom duxelles evenly to the edges of the spinach and then lay the beef fillet horizontally across the bottom of the mushrooms.

Using the clingfilm, roll everything into a tight parcel with the bresaola encasing the spinach, mushrooms and meat. Just before the clingfilm comes round to meet itself, neatly tuck in the ends of the bresaola. Continue rolling the parcel, making sure the clingfilm doesn't tuck into the bresaola. Fold over the ends of the clingfilm so it is airtight.

Lay the whole parcel down onto more clingfilm and wrap tightly. This will form the wellington into a neat cylinder shape and centre everything inside. Chill in the refrigerator overnight.

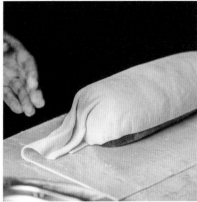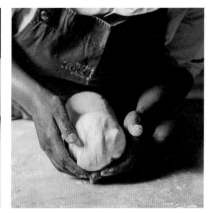

DAY TWO

Line a large baking tray with parchment paper. On a lightly floured surface, roll out the 300g of pastry for the lattice to a 40cm x 14cm rectangle. Slide he rolled-out pastry onto the lined tray, cover with clingfilm and chill in the refrigerator for 30 minutes.

On a lightly floured surface, roll out the 500g of pastry for the wellington to a 50cm x 35cm rectangle, no more than 5mm thick. Trim away any excess pastry. Dust off any excess flour from the pastry and then brush lightly all over with egg wash.

Carefully remove the wellington filling from the clingfilm using sharp scissors, taking care not to snip into the bresaola wrapping. Swiftly lift the filling as though cradling a baby (yes, a baby) and place it centred against the bottom edge of pastry closest to you. Lift up the bottom edge of the pastry against the filling and roll upwards until the filling is encased in pastry with a 4cm overlap. Make sure the seam of pastry runs directly along the bottom of the wellington.

Carefully flatten the loose ends down onto the work surface, thinning the pastry as much as possible but without tearing it. Leaving just enough to tuck under the wellington, trim away the excess pastry.

Line a large baking tray with parchment paper. Cradling it at either end, quickly transfer the wellington to the lined tray. Dust off any excess flour from the outside of the wellington and then brush it all over with egg wash. At this point, it is important not to rest the pastry – this is an opportunity to let the tautness of the gluten work for you as the pastry will shrink tightly against the filling inside providing a nicer cut-through.

...continued on page 202

  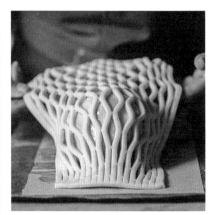

Remove the rolled-out pastry for the lattice from the refrigerator and lay it flat on your work surface. Using a lattice pastry cutter roller, firmly roll up the length of the pastry. Using a small knife, work through each of the cuts made by the roller to make sure that they will open properly when lightly stretched.

Turn the tray so that the wellington is at a right angle to you and give it another light brushing of egg wash. Gently stretch out the lattice pastry and lay it over the top of the wellington, stretching it evenly from the middle outwards until the lattice goes all the way down the sides of the wellington and can be tucked under. It is important that the lattice tucks all the way under or it will ride up the sides of the wellington during the cooking. Lightly brush the lattice with egg wash, taking care not to let the egg pool in the diamond-shaped gaps. Chill in the refrigerator for 30 minutes.

Preheat the oven to 200°C fan/220°C/gas mark 7.

Immediately before cooking, remove the wellington from the refrigerator, and give it a final egg wash and sprinkle over the sea salt. If you are feeling fancy, place a small thyme flower in the centre of each diamond of the lattice.

Place the tray in the preheated oven and bake the wellington for 30 minutes. After 30 minutes, turn the tray around inside the oven and then, referring to the timing guidelines below, take the meat to the correct temperature according to how you like your beef cooked. If you don't have a digital probe thermometer, cook the wellington for 45 minutes to achieve medium rare. But honestly, buy a probe.

Transfer the wellington to a wire cooling rack (this will allow air to circulate under the pastry and prevent it getting soggy) and rest for a minimum of 30 minutes before serving. Using a serrated knife, slice into 3cm thick portions. While slicing, look down from above the wellington to get an even cut.

COOKING GUIDE

Insert a digital probe thermometer into the middle of the wellington through one of the ends to check the temperature of the meat. Bear in mind that these cooking temperatures factor in that the temperature will continue to rise during the resting period.

For medium rare:
Cook to 36°C. The temperature will rise to 45°C while resting.
For medium:
Cook to 48°C. The temperature will rise to 52–55°C while resting.
For medium well:
Cook to 60°C. The temperature will rise to 65–70°C while resting.
For well done:
Buy a sausage roll and save yourself the hassle.

Coronation Chicken Pie

First created to honour the coronation of Queen Elizabeth II, this dish was devised by two principals of the Cordon Bleu cookery school in London. The original recipe was a creamy curried chicken with sultanas, still fairly light on spice (more suited to the tastes in Britain at the time) but full of flavour. Served cold as part of a buffet, this decorative coronation chicken pie looks incredible on the table at a party. It is worth investing in an oval pie mould, which can either be bought new online or from vintage suppliers. If possible, buy a mould with a fluted design as they look spectacular when you unmould your pie.

SERVES 8–10

800g shortcrust pastry (see
  page 56, or shop-bought)
10g butter, softened
1 egg yolk beaten with
  1 teaspoon water,
  for brushing

For the pie filling

10g black mustard seeds
1 tablespoon ground turmeric
2 teaspoons garam masala
1 teaspoon ground coriander
1 teaspoon ground cumin
6 skinless, boneless
  chicken thighs
40g fresh coriander, stalks and
  leaves roughly chopped
20g table salt
2 skinless chicken breasts, cut
  into 3cm dice
100g sultanas
2 red chillies, deseeded and
  finely chopped

For the mango jelly

6 gelatine leaves
500ml mango juice

On a lightly floured surface, roll out the pastry to a 5mm thick large rectangle. Cutting diagonally from corner to corner, cut a pastry strip 20cm wide and at least 50cm long, squaring off the ends. Lay the pastry strip on a large piece of parchment paper, folding the pastry if necessary, and chill in the refrigerator until needed.

Unclip the pie mould and take it apart. Using the shape of the pie mould as a guide, cut out two ovals from the resulting triangles of pastry, reserving any trimmings for decoration.

Re-assemble the pie mould and secure it with the clips. Brush the inside of the mould with the softened butter. Remove the strip of pastry from the refrigerator, gently fold it into a loop and carefully place it inside the greased mould. Let the bottom 2cm of the pastry strip slide down onto the base of the mould and flatten down. Next, press the pastry strip against the sides of the mould following the fluted shape. There should be a substantial overhang of pastry at the top of the mould, which you can ease over the top edge by making small snips in the pastry at either pointed end of the mould. After pressing the sides in, make sure the seam where the two ends of the pastry strip meet is no more than a 2cm overlap. Trim any excess pastry with scissors, if necessary, then push the ends firmly together.

Take one of the pastry ovals, trim 1cm from all the way round the edge and lay it on the base of the mould. Push the pastry oval against the mould and into the pastry strip where it overlaps the base to join the two. Put the pastry-lined mould into the refrigerator with the remaining pastry oval and any trimmings for decoration and chill for 30 minutes.

Meanwhile, make the filling. Preheat the oven to 190°C fan/210°C/gas mark 7. Spread the mustard seeds and ground spices over a baking tray and toast in the preheated oven for 8 minutes.

Put the chicken thighs in a food processor along with the fresh coriander and salt. Pulse until almost smooth. Transfer the mixture to a bowl, add the toasted spices, mix well and then fold in the diced chicken breast, sultanas and chilli.

Remove the pastry-lined mould from the refrigerator and fill with the chicken mixture to 1cm below the top edge of the pastry. Lay the remaining pastry oval over the top of the filling and crimp together with the overhanging pastry from the sides (see page 32). Return the mould to the refrigerator and chill for 20 minutes.

Preheat the oven to 190°C fan/210°C/gas mark 7.

Remove the mould from the refrigerator and cut a 2cm hole in the middle of the pie lid to allow steam to escape. Decorate the top of the pie however you prefer (see page 33). I added a paisley design, which is often found on shawls from Kashmir in India, as a suggestion as to the flavours found inside. Lightly brush the pastry all over with egg wash and then return to the refrigerator to chill for 20 minutes. When ready to bake, remove the pie from the refrigerator and brush again with the egg wash.

Place the mould in the preheated oven and bake the pie for 1–1¼ hours or until the pastry is a deep golden brown and the core temperature of the filling reads 63°C or above on a digital probe thermometer. Remove the pie from the oven and leave to cool completely in the mould on a wire rack and then refrigerate overnight.

Put the gelatine leaves in a small bowl and cover with cold water. Meanwhile, pour the mango juice into a small pan and warm over a low heat. After 3 minutes remove the gelatine from the bowl and squeeze out any excess water. Add the gelatine to the mango juice and whisk well until fully dissolved.

Using a small funnel or squeezy bottle, fill the pie with the mango jelly through the steam hole. Place the pie in the refrigerator and chill for a further 30 minutes before taking the pie out of the mould and serving.

Equipment
fluted oval game pie mould (24cm long and 8cm deep) and digital probe thermometer

PUDDINGS

Orange & Golden Syrup Steamed Pudding

Adding orange zest to a steamed pudding gives a little acidity to cut through the richness and also the most incredible aroma when it's served at the dining table.

--- SERVES 4 ---

Grease a 1.2-litre (2-pint) pudding basin with butter and place a small circle of parchment paper in the bottom. Firmly press the paper down into the base, avoiding making any creases. Pour half the golden syrup into the basin.

In a bowl, whisk the remaining syrup together with the butter, sugar and orange zest until creamy and forming soft peaks. Whisk in half the beaten eggs and then fold in half the flour. Repeat until all the eggs and flour are combined. Whisk in the milk and continue whisking for 1 minute until the batter is thick and creamy. Pour the batter into the basin, then level and smooth the surface with a spatula.

Cut two circles of parchment paper and a circle of aluminium foil twice the diameter of the top of the basin. Place the foil on top of both layers of parchment paper and make one 2cm wide pleat directly across the middle of the circle. Lay them across the top of the pudding basin. Using a length of string, secure the paper and foil firmly around the neck of the basin, then make one tie of string across the top to act as a handle. Make sure the string is tightly tied and secure as you don't want it to break while lifting.

Take a pan with a lid that is large enough to hold the pudding basin with a little space around the sides. Fill the pan with enough water to reach three-quarters of the way only up the side of the basin. Bring the water up to a boil and then carefully lower in the pudding basin, making sure that the water does not touch the paper and foil lid and put the lid on the pan. Lower the heat to a simmer and gently steam the pudding for 1½ hours. Do not remove the lid from the pan during the first 30 minutes of cooking as the drop in temperature may cause the pudding to collapse. After at least 30 minutes, check the water level in the pan at regular intervals and, if necessary, top up with boiling water from the kettle, taking care not to pour water onto the foil and paper lid. To check if the pudding is cooked, insert a skewer into the centre through the lid. If the skewer comes out clean, the pudding is ready. If the skewer has some batter on it, return the pudding to the pan and steam further until ready.

Allow the pudding to rest for 5 minutes and then remove the foil and paper lid. Using a thin knife, carefully work around the top edge of the basin to loosen the pudding so that it will come away from the basin easily. Invert a plate on top of the basin and, using a clean dish towel to protect your hands, quickly flip the whole thing over and lift off the pudding basin. Pour the extra 30g of golden syrup over the top of the pudding. Serve with a jug of custard.

110g golden syrup, plus an
    extra 30g for serving
190g butter, softened, plus an
    extra 10g for greasing
130g soft brown sugar
zest of 2 oranges
3 eggs, beaten
180g self-raising flour, sifted
20ml whole milk
Custard, to serve
    (see page 261)

Equipment
1.2-litre (2 pint) pudding basin

Panettone & Gianduja Pudding

This started as a very naughty Christmas indulgence, fuelled by gifts from the Italian chefs in my team. I would make toasted panettone and, while still warm, smother it with soft gianduja spread – a hazelnut and chocolate paste. While that is perfect for feeding the family on Boxing Day evening, snuggled up in front of a film, turning it into a bread and butter pudding is an easy next step, and now it's one of the most comforting dishes I know. While panettone is generally easy to find, I sometimes struggle to find soft gianduja. You can replace it with another chocolate and hazelnut spread that is more widely available, but use the original whenever you can – the real hazelnuts make a big difference in flavour.

SERVES 4

350g panettone (about half a medium panettone)
60g butter
100g gianduja (or other chocolate and hazelnut spread)
2 eggs, beaten
150ml double cream
200ml whole milk
20g caster sugar
1 vanilla pod
10g icing sugar, to decorate

Equipment
850ml (1½-pint) ovenproof dish

Preheat the oven to 170°C fan/190°C/gas mark 5.

Using a serrated knife, and leaving the crust on, cut the panettone into medium thickness slices and then again into wedges. Lay the panettone wedges over an oven tray. Place the tray in the preheated oven and bake the panettone for 10 minutes or until starting to harden.

Butter one side of the panettone wedges with 50g of the butter and then spread the gianduja across the same sides.

Grease an 850ml (1½-pint) ovenproof dish with the remaining 10g of butter and then arrange the panettone wedges, butter and gianduja side up, neatly inside.

Combine the egg, cream, milk and sugar in a bowl. Split the vanilla pod lengthways and scrape the seeds into the bowl. Stir together until the sugar has dissolved and then pour the mixture over the panettone, enusre you coat everything evenly.

Place the ovenproof dish in a roasting tray and fill the tray with boiling water from the kettle to halfway up the sides of the dish. Cook for 40 minutes. The top of the pudding should be golden and crusty at the end of cooking; if not cook until achieved then dust with the icing sugar to serve.

I prefer to eat this just by itself, while still warm, so let it rest for 10 minutes before serving.

Apricot & Lemon Thyme Cobblers

This dish combines two of my favourite desserts: fruit crumble and fruit tart. It brings back memories of working at a restaurant in Alberta, Canada just after I'd left school, where we served this dish. Some cobbler tops look a little dumpling-like, while others are more of an open crumble – this falls firmly in the latter camp. The British in me implores you to serve this dessert with custard, but it works just as well when a ball of vanilla ice cream is left to melt on top of the hot cobbler. This recipes makes enough for 12 individual cobblers, so you can either serve two cobblers per person or freeze any that you aren't going to use.

SERVES 6

Preheat the oven to 160°C fan/180°C/gas mark 4 and line two baking trays with parchment paper. On a lightly floured surface, roll out the pastry to a thickness of 1.5cm. Cut out six pastry circles large enough to line the cups of the muffin tray. To line the cups, carefully place the pastry circles in the cups, leaving no air bubbles and pushing down any creases. Place the muffin tray in the freezer and chill the pastry cases for 30 minutes or until hard.

While the pastry cases are chilling, put all the ingredients for the crumble mixture in a mixing bowl and gently rub together until just combined. Spread the crumble mixture over the first lined baking tray. Lay the apricot halves on the second lined baking tray, flat side down.

Remove the muffin tray from the freezer. Line each pastry case with a circle of parchment paper and then fill with ceramic baking beans or dried pulses or rice.

Place the muffin tray and both baking trays in the preheated oven to blind bake the pastry cases and roast the crumble mixture and the apricots for 20 minutes. After the first 10 minutes, carefully turn over each apricot half and gently move around the crumble mixture with a spoon so everything cooks evenly. After the full 20 minutes remove both baking trays from the oven and set aside to cool a little. Remove the muffin tray from the oven. Lift out the parchment paper from the pastry cases to remove the baking beans. Increase the oven temperature to 180°C fan/200°C/gas mark 6, return the muffin tray to the oven and cook the pastry cases for a further 5 minutes or until an even golden colour. Remove the muffin tray from the oven and set aside.

Transfer the apricots to a mixing bowl and, while still warm, sprinkle over the caster sugar and scrape in the vanilla seeds from the pod. Stir everything together, gently breaking up the apricots while stirring. Spoon the apricot mixture into the tart cases. Loosely scatter the crumble mix over the top of each filled tart case and then finally add the picked lemon thyme leaves to decorate the cobblers. Serve immediately while warm with either custard or ice cream.

500g sweet shortcrust pastry (see page 58)
15 apricots, halved and stone removed
60g caster sugar
1 vanilla pod
20g lemon thyme, leaves picked

For the crumble
100g plain flour
80g cold salted butter, diced
80g caster sugar
80g ground almonds
10g flaked almonds

Equipment
6-hole, non-stick muffin tray

Glazed Apple Tart

The slightly more elegant sibling of the classic apple pie, this tart is a stunning
dessert. It has similar flavours to a tarte tatin as the sugar caramelises as it cooks.
You could serve this tart with clotted cream to balance the sweetness of the apples.

SERVES 6

300g classic puff pastry (see
page 63 or shop-bought)
200g Frangipane
(see page 261)
80g caster sugar
80g unsalted butter, softened
6–8 Pink Lady or Granny
Smith apples
20g icing sugar
clotted cream, to serve

Line a baking tray with parchment paper. On a lightly floured surface, roll out
the pastry into a large circle about 5mm thick. Slide the rolled-out pastry onto
the lined baking tray and rest in the refrigerator for 15 minutes or in the freezer
for 10 minutes. Remove the tray from the refrigerator or freezer. Trim the edges
of the pastry into a neat circle that measures 24cm in diameter and return to the
refrigerator or freezer.

Once chilled, remove the pastry from the refrigerator or freezer, and preheat
the oven to 185°C fan/200°C/gas mark 6. With the pastry still on the lined baking
tray, and leaving a border of 2cm around the edge, spread the frangipane evenly
across the pastry.

Using a pastry brush, mix the caster sugar and softened butter together to
make a paste.

Peel and core the apples. Using a mandoline, slice the apples to 2mm thick.
Take just over one-quarter of the slices and fan them out in a circle around the
outer edge, keeping in line with the edge of the frangipane. Roughly brush the
apples with some of the butter mixture. Repeat with the remaining apple slices
and butter mixture to create concentric circles until the pastry is covered. Make
sure the top layer of apple slices is evenly coated with the butter mixture.

Place the tray in the preheated oven and bake the tart for 30 minutes or until
the apples are starting to caramelise and the pastry is beginning to crisp up.

Remove the tray from the oven. Using a sieve, dust the tart with the icing sugar
and then lay another sheet of parchment paper over the top of the apples. Take
a second baking tray and lay it on top of that parchment paper. Using a dish towel
or oven gloves to protect your hands, quickly flip the tart over so the apples are
now facing downwards on the new tray. Lightly press down the top tray and then
remove it and the original parchment paper. Return the tart to the oven for a
further 20 minutes.

Remove the tart from the oven. This time place a serving plate or platter on top
of the pastry, and then flip the tart again. Check the apples are evenly glazed and
caramelised. If it needs a little longer, flip the tart back again and return it to the
oven for a further 10 minutes. Serve warm with spoonfuls of clotted cream.

Rhubarb & Custard Tart

This tart is best made when forced Yorkshire rhubarb is at its peak, around mid-January to March. In season, forced rhubarb is a stunning, bright pink fruit. Out of season, rhubarb is still a delight and if you really want that lurid pink colour you can always add a touch of grenadine to the poaching liquid when you cook the fruit. An absolute rule at the restaurant is that, be it chocolate, custard or lemon, we never serve a tart that has been in a refrigerator as it completely changes its texture and fragrance. Anything left over at the end of a service is finished up by the team, so what is served the next day to diners is always fresh from the oven. I apply the same principle at home, explaining to my wife that we 'have' to finish the tart because rules are rules.

SERVES 4

400g sweet shortcrust pastry
(see page 58)
10g butter, for greasing
1 egg yolk beaten with
1 teaspoon of water,
for glazing
2 lemon thyme sprigs
(optional), leaves picked,
for decorating

For the custard
150ml whole milk
150ml double cream
70g golden caster sugar
1 vanilla pod
2 eggs, beaten

For the rhubarb
500g rhubarb
zest and juice of 1 orange
30g caster sugar

Equipment
35cm x 12cm rectangular tart
tin with a removable base

Roll out the pastry to 5mm thick and to fit the tart tin with a small overlap of 2cm. Grease the tin with the butter and line with the pastry, making sure it goes well into the edges. Place the pastry-lined tin in the refrigerator to chill for 30 minutes.

Preheat the oven to 180°C fan/200°C/gas mark 6.

Remove the tin from the refrigerator, make sure the pastry is still neatly tucked into the edges and prick the base all over. Lay a sheet of parchment paper inside the pastry case and then fill with baking beans. Bake for 12 minutes then remove the baking beans and cook for a further 5 minutes. The pastry should be golden brown but not dark; if not bake a further few minutes until golden then remove from the oven. Lightly brush the surface of the pastry all over with the egg wash, covering well any hairline cracks, and return to the oven for 2 minutes. Remove the tart case from the oven and set aside.

Lower the oven temperature to 150°C fan/170°C/gas mark 3.

Meanwhile, make the custard. Combine the milk, cream and golden caster sugar in a pan. Split open the vanilla pod and scrape the seeds into the pan and bring everything to a simmer over a medium heat. Put the beaten eggs into a mixing bowl and, whisking continuously and vigorously, gradually pour in the hot milk and cream mixture until well combined. Transfer the custard to a jug.

Place the pastry case on an oven tray inside the oven. Carefully pour the custard from the jug into the pastry case to three-quarters of the way up the sides. Bake the tart for 25 minutes. To check the tart is cooked, wiggle the tray. If it looks fairly set but still has a tiny wobble in the middle, it's perfect. If not, continue to cook further in 5-minute intervals, checking each time to see if it needs a little longer. Remove the tart from the oven and set aside to cool in the tin.

While the tart is cooling, prepare the rhubarb. Peel the rhubarb stalks and place the peelings in a medium pan with the orange zest and juice, caster sugar and 30ml water, and then gently warm until the sugar has dissolved. Strain the syrup through a sieve into a bowl, squeezing any liquid from the pulp left behind, and return the syrup to the pan.

Cut the rhubarb stalks into 6cm long batons and divide into two batches. Bring the syrup up to a simmer and drop in the first batch of rhubarb and cook just for 1 minute until softened. Carefully remove the rhubarb from the pan with a spatula or slotted spoon and leave to dry on paper towels. Repeat with the second batch of rhubarb. Increase the heat under the syrup and reduce to the consistency of a glaze.

Arrange the rhubarb batons across the top of the custard in two vertical columns to fill the tart case, then lightly brush the fruit with the sticky syrup to glaze.

When the tart has fully cooled (45 minutes to 1 hour after being removed from the oven), carefully unmould the tart from the tin. To finish, garnish the tart with picked lemon thyme leaves, if using.

Pecan & Frangipane Tart

The addition of pecans, gently caramelised in a little honey, turns a simple, classic tart into something almost impossible to stop eating. I've always found frangipane to be light, so it can take the additional richness without ruining what becomes a decadent dish. Serve slices of this tart with a little fruit and something creamy to bind everything together; here I've suggested fresh raspberries and clotted cream.

SERVES 6-8

On a lightly floured surface, roll out the pastry dough into a large disc 1cm thick, then place on a parchment-lined tray to rest in the refrigerator for 30 minutes or in the freezer for 15 minutes.

Grease the inside of the tart tin with 5g of the butter and then line it with the chilled disc of pastry. To do this, roll the pastry around the rolling pin and lay it carefully over the tin. Press the pastry firmly against the sides of the tin and into the corners. Using a fork, prick the base of the pastry case all over. Put it in the refrigerator for 20 minutes.

Preheat the oven to 190°C fan/210°C/gas mark 6½. Once rested, trim away any excess pastry from the top edge of the tin. Line the pastry case with baking parchment and fill with ceramic baking beans. Bake in the preheated oven for 15 minutes.

Meanwhile, line a baking tray with baking parchment. Mix the pecans with the honey and spread them across the lined baking tray. Remove the baking beans and parchment from the pastry case and return to the oven along with the tray of pecans for a further 10 minutes. Take the tart case and the nuts out of the oven and allow to cool for 10 minutes. Lower the oven temperature to 180°C fan/200°C/Gas Mark 6.

While the pastry and nuts are cooling, whisk together the butter and sugar until pale (about 10 minutes by hand or 5 minutes with an electric mixer). Gradually add the eggs, slowly whisking them in, and then stir in the ground almonds.

Pour the frangipane mixture into the pastry case. Evenly spread the pecans over the top, pushing them down into the filling, and then scatter the flaked almonds all over. Place the tin in the hot oven and bake the tart for 35 minutes or until the frangipane has risen and is golden in colour.

Carefully remove the tart from the tin by setting it over a bowl smaller than the hole in the base and allowing the sides of the tin to drop away. Lightly dust the tart with icing sugar. Serve while still warm with a handful of raspberries and some clotted cream on the side.

400g sweet shortcrust pastry (see page 58)
5g butter, softened

For the pecan frangipane
200g pecans
1 tablespoon runny honey
110g butter, softened
110g caster sugar
3 medium eggs, beaten
110g ground almonds
25g flaked almonds

To serve
icing sugar, to dust
raspberries
clotted cream

Equipment
24cm diameter loose-bottomed fluted tart tin

Fig, Honey & Pistachio Clafoutis

When figs are at their best, plump and ripe, teaming them up with pistachio nuts and honey makes for a beautiful pudding. The first key step to a great clafoutis is to reduce the water content of the fruit before adding it to the batter, so it doesn't seep into the pudding as it cooks, resulting in a better structure. My second tip is to brown the butter, which adds a nuttiness to the whole dish.

―――――――――――――― SERVES 4 ――――――――――――――

8 ripe figs
60g caster sugar
30g butter
2 eggs, beaten
1 vanilla pod
20g plain flour, sifted
4 tablespoons whole milk
4 tablespoons double cream
25g shelled pistachios,
     roughly chopped
2 tablespoons runny honey
10g icing sugar, to decorate
clotted cream, to serve

Equipment
20cm oval ovenproof dish

Preheat the oven to 200°C fan/220°C/gas mark 7 and line a large baking tray with parchment paper.

Using a sharp knife, slice the figs in half lengthways. Lay the figs on the lined baking tray, cut side up, and dust with 10g of the caster sugar. Place the tray in the preheated oven and roast for 12 minutes. Remove the tray from the oven and set aside to cool. Reduce the oven temperature to 180°C fan/200°C/gas mark 6.

Meanwhile, melt 20g of the butter in a small saucepan over a medium heat until it just starts to brown – remove the pan from the heat as soon as you see the colour change and do not allow the butter to blacken. Pour the browned butter into a small bowl to stop the cooking process and leave to cool slightly.

Put the beaten eggs into a mixing bowl. Split the vanilla pod lengthways and scrape the seeds into the eggs. Add the remaining caster sugar to the eggs and whisk for at least 5 minutes until the eggs have taken in plenty of air and have increased in volume.

Using a silicone spatula, fold the flour into the egg mixture until fully incorporated, but avoid knocking out all the air. Finally, fold the browned butter, milk and cream into the mixture to make the clafoutis batter.

Butter a 20cm ovenproof dish with the remaining 10g of butter. Pour the clafoutis batter into the dish and nestle the roasted figs in the batter. Place the ovenproof dish in the hot oven and bake the clafoutis for 25 minutes.

Remove the dish from the oven and scatter the chopped pistachios over the top of the clafoutis. Turn the dish around before putting it back in the oven for a further 15 minutes. At the end of the cooking time, the centre of the clafoutis should be risen. If it is still dipped, cook the clafoutis for a further 5 minutes or until it rises. Leave the pudding to stand for 10 minutes before serving.

When ready to serve, drizzle the clafoutis all over with the runny honey and dust with the icing sugar. A small bowl of clotted cream served on the side to accompany the clafoutis is perfect.

PERFECT
SIDE DISHES

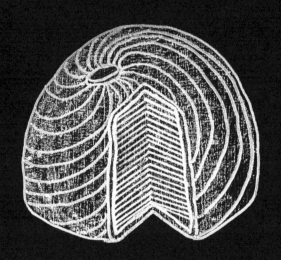

Clockwise from top left:

Confit Duck Hash (page 233),
Bubble & Squeak (page 235),
Perfect Hasselback Potatoes (page
234), Clapshot (page 232) and
Braised Red Cabbage (page 232)

Clapshot

600g swede, peeled and cut
   into 2cm dice
450g King Edward or Maris
   Piper potatoes, peeled and
   cut into 2cm dice
80g butter, softened
4 tablespoons hot milk
2 thyme sprigs, leaves picked
1/3 teaspoon table salt
1/3 teaspoon freshly ground
   black pepper

In separate pans, boil the diced swede and the potatoes until tender and easily pierced with the tip of a sharp knife. The swede and potatoes will have different cooking times: I cook the swede for 25 minutes and the potatoes for 15 minutes. Drain both the swede and potato well and combine in a single pan.

Add the butter, milk, thyme, salt and pepper to the pan and then roughly mash with a potato masher or a fork. Do not overwork the clapshot as it is nicer to eat when it retains a little texture.

Braised Red Cabbage

1/2 large red cabbage (around
   600g), core removed and
   leaves finely shredded
2 Spanish onions, peeled
   and sliced
1 cooking apple, peeled
   and grated
2 tablespoons soft brown sugar
20ml white wine vinegar
20ml olive oil
20g butter
150ml red wine
1/2 cinnamon stick
1/4 nutmeg, grated
1/2 teaspoon table salt

Place all the ingredients in a large pan with a lid. Bring the liquid to the boil then reduce the heat to a simmer and put a lid on the pan. Cook the cabbage for 1 1/2 hours, stirring every 20–30 minutes. After 1 1/2 hours, take the lid off the pan and cook until the liquid has evaporated.

Confit Duck Hash

Duck hash is a versatile number: it can be served on the side as part of a roast, on its own as a main course with some vegetables and a little mustard sauce, or even topped with poached or fried eggs. The secret to its golden colour is the removal of the moisture from the potatoes, so make sure you really squeeze well at that stage.

MAKES 8 (ENOUGH FOR 8 PEOPLE AS A SIDE OR 4 PEOPLE AS A MAIN)

Preheat the oven to 160°C fan/180°C/gas mark 4. Take a small heavy-based pan with a lid in which the duck legs fit neatly, cover the base of the pan with a circle of parchment paper and put the duck fat on top. Place the pan in the preheated oven for 5 minutes to melt the fat and then carefully lay the duck legs in the pan. Lay another circle of parchment paper on top to cover the duck and place the lid on top.

Place the pan back in the oven and cook the duck legs for 1½ hours. Carefully remove the lid and check that the meat is soft and tender. If it still has a little resistance and doesn't fall away from the bone, put the duck back in the oven to cook for a further 20 minutes and then check again. Once the meat is ready, transfer the duck legs to a plate to cool. Set aside the pan with the rendered duck fat to use later (any duck fat left over can be used for roasting potatoes or vegetables and kept in the refrigerator for up to one month). Increase the oven temperature to 180°C fan/200°C/gas mark 6.

Using the large holes on a box grater, grate the potatoes into a bowl. Add the table salt to the grated potato and mix well. Transfer the potato to a sieve and sit it above the bowl. Allow any liquid to drain from the potatoes for 10 minutes. Using a clean dish towel, take a small handful of the potato mixture and squeeze to remove any remaining moisture. Repeat with the rest of the potato mixture.

In a separate bowl, combine the potato with 150g of the melted duck fat and mix well. Add the rosemary and season with lots of freshly ground black pepper.

Once cooled, remove all the meat from the duck legs, discarding the bones and skin. Without breaking it down too much, distribute the duck meat through the potato. Divide the hash mixture into eight equal piles on a tray.

Place a frying pan over a medium heat and heat up a large tablespoon of the remaining duck fat. Carefully lower three of the hash piles into the hot fat and gently pat each one down with a spatula, but don't squash them down too much or they will become too dense. Cook the hash for about 3 minutes on each side. The potato should be golden brown; if not cook for another minute or so on each side. Return the cooked hash to the tray and repeat with the other hash piles. Put the tray in the preheated oven for 10 minutes before serving.

2 duck legs
500g duck fat
1.2kg large roasting
    potatoes, peeled
2 teaspoons table salt
2 rosemary sprigs, leaves
    picked and finely chopped
freshly ground black pepper

Perfect Hasselback Potatoes

1kg medium King Edward
    potatoes or other floury
    variety, unpeeled
40ml vegetable oil
60g salted butter
¾ teaspoon table salt
2 rosemary sprigs
½ bunch thyme
2 garlic cloves, lightly crushed

Either the night before or on the morning of the meal, prepare the potatoes. Trim an edge off one long side of each potato so they sit steadily on the chopping board. About 1cm up from the flat edge, poke a long skewer lengthways into a potato all the way through to the other side. The skewer acts as a guide for evenly cutting the potato. First, slice straight across the middle of the potato and then make more cuts along to both ends, each 3mm apart and on a slight angle away from the centre cut, slicing all the way down to the skewer each time. This will allow the potato to open up as it cooks. Remove the skewer and repeat with the rest of the potatoes.

Put the prepared potatoes into a large container and place under cold running water for 5 minutes. Next, fill the container to the brim with water and place in the refrigerator until needed.

When ready to cook, preheat the oven to 190°C fan/210°C/gas mark 6½.

Remove the container from the refrigerator and drain the potatoes well. Take a roasting tray that is large enough to fit all the potatoes, add the oil and butter to the tray and place in the preheated oven for a few minutes until melted. Carefully lower the potatoes into the tray, flat side down, being careful not to splash yourself with the hot fat. Return the tray to the oven and roast the potatoes for 20 minutes.

After 20 minutes, baste the potatoes well, sprinkle the salt over evenly and roast them for a further 15 minutes. Baste the potatoes again, this time adding the rosemary, thyme and garlic, and roast for a further 15 minutes. Baste the potatoes for a final time, before transferring to a serving dish.

Bubble & Squeak

Place the potatoes in a pan and cover with water. Bring to the boil over a high heat and cook for 15–20 minutes or until tender.

Meanwhile, heat 1 tablespoon of the vegetable oil in a frying pan over a medium heat. Add the onions and sauté, stirring occasionally, for 10 minutes. Add the diced carrots to the pan with the butter and 1 tablespoon of water, then cook for a further 5 minutes. Lastly, add the sliced cabbage and 1 tablespoon of water and cook for a further 3 minutes, stirring occasionally. Line a plate with paper towels and transfer the vegetables onto the plate to cool.

When the potatoes are tender, place them in a colander and allow to drain well. Return the potatoes to the pan and mash well with a potato masher. Add the cooled vegetables, rosemary, salt and a good few twists of freshly ground black pepper and combine well.

Once the mixture has cooled, divide it equally into six portions and shape into patties. Dust the tops and bottoms of each 'bubble' with a little of the flour.

Preheat the oven to 180°C fan/200°C/gas mark 6 and line a baking tray with parchment paper.

Wipe clean the frying pan, place over a high heat and add the remaining vegetable oil. Cooking them in batches so as not to overcrowd the pan, carefully slide three bubbles into the oil and shallow fry for 2 minutes on each side until they have a golden crust. Transfer the fried bubbles to the tray. Cook the remaining bubbles in the same way.

Place the tray in the preheated oven and bake the bubbles for 10 minutes to make sure they are thoroughly hot inside.

500g Maris Piper or King
    Edward potatoes, peeled
    and quartered
2 tablespoons vegetable oil
1 Spanish onion, peeled
    and sliced
100g carrots, diced
10g butter
¼ Savoy cabbage, finely sliced
2 rosemary sprigs, leaves
    picked and roughly chopped
10g table salt
10g plain flour
freshly ground black pepper

Clockwise from top left:

Rarebit Baked Potato (page 239), Slow-Roasted Carrots & Cumin (page 242), Sweetcorn & Chickpea Fritters (page 241), Celeriac & Apple Remoulade (page 238) and Minted Bean Salad (page 240)

Perfect Mash

Perfect mash to me is just potato, good butter and seasoning, nothing else.

SERVES 4

1kg Desiree or Maris
    Piper potatoes
100g good-quality butter
sea salt and freshly ground
    black pepper

Peel the potatoes and cut them into quarters. Rinse in a medium-sized saucepan under cold water for 1 minute to remove some of the starch, then just cover with water. Add 1 teaspoon of salt, place over a high heat and bring to the boil.

Reduce to a simmer and cook until a knife easily slips into the centre of each potato (roughly 15 minutes). Strain in a colander and allow to steam off for a few minutes. Tip back into the saucepan and either break the potatoes down with a potato ricer (my preferred method) or a masher.

Put the pan over a low heat, add the butter and mix until well incorporated. Finish with plenty of black pepper and a touch of salt if it needs it.

Celeriac & Apple Remoulade

SERVES 6–8
---

1 small celeriac, peeled
    and quartered
4 Granny Smith apples
50g Mayonnaise
    (see page 260)
3 tablespoons English mustard
2 tablespoons wholegrain
    mustard
2 tablespoons cider vinegar
¼ bunch parsley, chopped
¾ teaspoon table salt
freshly ground black pepper

Using a mandoline, very carefully slice the celeriac quarters into 3mm slices. Arrange the slices into small stacks and slice into thin matchsticks.

Without peeling them and avoiding their cores, slice the apples on the mandoline to the same thickness as the celeriac. Likewise, cut the apple slices into thin matchsticks.

Combine the mayonnaise, mustards, vinegar and parsley in a bowl and mix well. Fold the celeriac and apple matchsticks through the mayonnaise mixture and then season with the salt and a little freshly ground black pepper. Taste and adjust the seasoning, adding a little more salt, if necessary.

Rarebit Baked Potato

How do you improve on a simple baked potato? I've always felt that the best part is the crispy skin and the deep, savoury flavour that it takes on with a long bake, so we haven't changed that here. Instead, we've altered the mixture inside, adding a decadent topping to make this a really beautiful family dish. I serve this either as part of a feast or as a simple main dish with sliced ripe tomatoes dressed simply with olive oil and salt.

SERVES 6 AS A MAIN OR MANY AS PART OF A FEAST

Preheat the oven to 200°C fan/220°C/gas mark 7.

Place the potatoes on a baking tray, prick their tops a couple of times with a fork and then rub them all over with the vegetable oil. Place the tray in the centre of the preheated oven and bake for 1 hour or until the potatoes are soft when pierced with the tip of a knife.

Meanwhile, prepare the rarebit mixture. In a bowl, combine the beaten eggs, milk, flour, grated cheese, breadcrumbs, mustard, wine and Worcestershire sauce and mix well with a fork. Add the cayenne pepper and salt. Put the bowl in the refrigerator and chill the rarebit mixture while the potatoes finish baking.

When the potatoes are ready, allow them to cool for 5 minutes. Using a clean dish towel to protect your hands, turn the potatoes on their sides and cut off the flattest edge with a serrated knife to reveal the insides. Leaving just enough so the potatoes hold their structure, scoop out three-quarters of the insides into a bowl. Using a fork, mash the potato with the butter and cheese and season to taste. Refill the potato shells with the potato mixture.

Remove the rarebit mixture from the refrigerator and spread it across the tops of the baked potatoes. Return the tray to the oven and bake the potatoes for a further 15 minutes until the rarebit mixture is golden brown.

6 large King Edward potatoes
 or other floury variety
2 teaspoons vegetable oil
60g salted butter
200g Cheddar cheese, grated
sea salt and freshly ground
 black pepper

For the rarebit

3 eggs, beaten
140ml semi-skimmed milk
15g plain flour
200g Cheddar cheese, grated
50g white breadcrumbs
2 tablespoons English mustard
50ml white wine
3 teaspoons Worcestershire
 sauce
a pinch of cayenne pepper
⅓ teaspoon salt

Minted Bean Salad

300g runner beans
600g fine green beans
½ bunch mint, leaves picked
   and stalks reserved
4 teaspoons cider vinegar
1 teaspoon Dijon mustard
2 tablespoons extra-virgin
   olive oil
sea salt and freshly ground
   black pepper

Trim the tops off the runner beans and, using a vegetable peeler, shave a thin strip from both sides of each bean. Cut into 2.5cm diamond shapes. Cut the stalks off the green beans.

Place a bowl of iced water next to the stove. Bring a large pan of water to the boil with the mint stalks. Season with salt until the water is as salty as the sea. Add both types of bean to the pan and boil for 2½ minutes. Remove from the heat, drain the beans and mint stalks and then plunge them into the iced water and leave until cold. Drain again until the beans are dry, discarding the mint stalks.

Mix together the vinegar, mustard and olive oil to make a dressing, then toss the beans in the dressing. Season the beans with a little freshly ground black pepper and sea salt. Finally, finely slice the mint leaves and toss into the salad and serve.

Sweetcorn & Chickpea Fritters

Squeeze as much moisture as possible from the sweetcorn. Place three-quarters of the sweetcorn in a food processor with the chickpeas and pulse to a rough paste. Transfer the sweetcorn paste to a bowl and then fold through the remaining sweetcorn kernels, spring onions, flour, paprika, cumin and salt.

Weigh the fritter mixture into 50g portions. Roughly roll each portion into a ball, place on a tray and chill in the refrigerator for 15 minutes.

Preheat the oven to 190°C fan/210°C/gas mark 6½ and line a baking tray with parchment paper.

Once the fritter mixture is chilled, remove the tray from the refrigerator and shape the balls into patties. Dust the tops and bottoms of each fritter with a little of the flour.

Place a frying pan over a medium heat and add the vegetable oil. Cooking them in batches so as not to overcrowd the pan, carefully slide five fritters into the oil and shallow fry for 2 minutes on each side until they have a golden crust. Transfer the fried fritters to the parchment-lined baking tray. Cook the remaining fritters in the same way.

Place the tray in the preheated oven and bake the fritters for 10 minutes to make sure they are thoroughly hot inside.

300g drained
   sweetcorn kernels
200g drained chickpeas
1 bunch spring onions,
   finely sliced
30g gluten-free plain flour,
   plus extra for dusting
   (gluten-free flour results in
   a crispier fritter, but regular
   plain flour can also be used)
½ teaspoon paprika
1 teaspoon ground cumin
¾ teaspoon table salt
40ml vegetable oil

Slow-Roasted Carrots & Cumin

SERVES 6

9 large carrots
30ml vegetable oil
20g butter, softened
⅔ teaspoon table salt
1 teaspoon cumin seeds
3 garlic cloves

Preheat the oven to 180°C fan/200°C/gas mark 6 and line a small roasting tray with aluminium foil.

Wash the carrots well but leave them unpeeled. Trim the tops and split them in half lengthways.

Place a large frying pan over a medium heat. Warm the vegetable oil in the pan, add the halved carrots, flat side down and four at a time, and fry until well coloured.

Transfer the carrots to the foil-lined tray, brush them with the butter and sprinkle with the salt and cumin seeds. Lightly crush the garlic cloves and nestle them in between the carrots. Place the tray in the preheated oven and roast the carrots for 25 minutes.

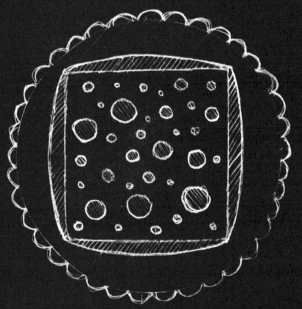

ACCOMPANIMENTS
SAUCES & BASICS

Clockwise from top left:

Piccalilli (page 249), IPA Wholegrain Mustard (page 251), Plum & Star Anise Chutney (page 248), Green Sauce (page 254), Tomato and Red Pepper Chutney (page 248)

Plum & Star Anise Chutney

MAKES 2 X 500ML JARS

600g plums, stoned and
quartered
2 Spanish onions, peeled
and finely diced
2 cooking apples, peeled
and grated
150ml cider vinegar
100g sultanas
150g soft brown sugar
4 star anise
200ml water

Equipment
2 x 500ml preserving jars

Place all the ingredients in a large saucepan and bring to the boil over a high heat. Once boiling, lower the heat and simmer for 45 minutes or until the chutney is thick and pulpy. Stir regularly with a wooden spoon throughout the cooking to make sure the chutney does not catch on the bottom of the pan.

To sterilise the jars, place them in a pan that is just large enough to hold them and cover with cold water. Bring the water to the boil and then allow the jars to cool in the water. Using clean tongs, remove the jars from the pan of water and dry with a clean dish towel.

Remove the star anise from the chutney. Spoon the chutney into the sterilised jars and seal. The chutney will last for up to two weeks when stored in a jar and kept in the refrigerator. Alternatively, store in an airtight container in the freezer for up to six months.

Tomato & Red Pepper Chutney

MAKES 1 JAR OR ENOUGH FOR 10 SERVINGS

10ml vegetable oil
1 medium Spanish onion,
finely chopped
2g table salt
1 green chilli, deseeded and
finely chopped
1 garlic clove, finely chopped
400g canned tomatoes, drained
and juice reserved
200ml white wine vinegar
400g caster sugar
1 teaspoon nigella seeds
2 red peppers, deseeded and
chopped into 1cm dice

Equipment
1 x 500ml preserving jar

Heat the vegetable oil in a medium-sized saucepan over a medium heat for 1 minute then add the onion, salt, chilli and garlic and cook while stirring for 5 minutes until soft. Do not allow the onions to colour but turn down the heat if necessary. Add the tomato juice, vinegar and sugar and cook until the liquid has reduced by half.

Add the tomatoes, nigella seeds and peppers and cook for 1 hour on a very low heat until the chutney is well thickened and glossy.

Meanwhile, sterilise the preserving jar. Place the jar in a pan that is just large enough to hold it and cover with cold water. Bring the water to the boil and then allow the jar to cool in the water.

Using clean tongs, remove the preserving jar from the pan of water and dry with a clean dish towel. Fill the jar with the chutney, seal and leave for at least one day before using. The chutney will last for up to two months when sealed in the jar and stored in the refrigerator.

Piccalilli

Place the fennel, cauliflower florets, onions, beans and peppers in a large bowl. Heat 3 litres of water in a large pan with 300g table salt and whisk until just dissolved. Pour the hot salted water over the vegetables and leave to salt for 4 hours.

Meanwhile, sterilise the preserving jars. Place the jars in a pan that is just large enough to hold them and cover with cold water. Bring the water to the boil and then allow the jars to cool in the water.

After the vegetables have been salting for 4 hours, drain the vegetables and then rinse in cold running water. Leave to drain well.

Meanwhile, make the piccalilli mixture. Put all the ingredients in a large saucepan and, whisking slowly, cook over a low heat until thickened. Add the drained vegetables to the piccalilli mixture and stir to mix well.

Using clean tongs, remove the preserving jars from the pan of water and dry with a clean dish towel. Fill each jar with the piccalilli, seal and leave for at least one day before using. The piccalilli will last for up to two months when sealed in the jars and stored in the refrigerator.

1 fennel bulb, roughly chopped into 2cm chunks
1 cauliflower, cut into small florets
2 onions, roughly chopped into 2cm chunks
200g green beans, cut into small batons
1 red pepper, cut into 2cm dice
1 green pepper, cut into 2cm dice
300g table salt, for salting

For the piccalilli mixture
350ml cider vinegar
200ml water
3 tablespoons hot mustard powder
2 tablespoons cornflour
1 tablespoon ground turmeric
1 tablespoon cayenne pepper
1 teaspoon dried chilli flakes
2 teaspoons mustard seeds
3 tablespoons caster sugar
2 teaspoons salt

Equipment
4 x 500ml preserving jars

Old-School Mint Sauce

100g mint sprigs
750g caster sugar
50ml white wine vinegar
25ml red wine vinegar
10ml water
pinch of salt

Equipment
1 x 250ml preserving jar

To sterilise the jar, place it in a pan that is just large enough to hold it and cover with cold water. Bring the water to the boil and then allow the jar to cool in the water. Using clean tongs, remove the preserving jar from the pan of water and dry with a clean dish towel.

Pick the mint leaves from the stalks and set aside. Put the stalks in a small saucepan with the sugar, vinegars, water and salt. Bring to a boil over a high heat and remove the stalks, then add the mint leaves and cook for 2 minutes, stirring frequently until the leaves have softened and are well cooked.

Transfer the mixture to a food processor and pulse until the mint leaves have broken down but are not completely blended. Set the sauce in a bowl above iced water and stir until it has cooled.

Spoon the sauce into the sterilised jar and seal. The sauce will last for up to one week when stored in a jar and kept in the refrigerator.

IPA Wholegrain Mustard

Place the mustard seeds in a container at least twice the volume of the seeds themselves as they will swell and expand during soaking. Pour the beer and vinegar over the seeds and leave to soak for 48 hours.

To sterilise the jar, place it in a pan that is just large enough to hold it and cover with cold water. Bring the water to the boil and then allow the jar to cool in the water. Using clean tongs, remove the preserving jar from the pan of water and dry with a clean dish towel.

Place half the soaked mustard seeds in a food processor with the sugar and salt and blend until smooth. Transfer the smooth mustard mixture to a bowl, add the remaining whole mustard seeds and stir until well combined.

Spoon the mustard into the sterilised jar, seal and leave for a least one day before using. Ideally, leave the mustard in the refrigerator for two weeks to develop its flavour.

100g brown mustard seeds
50g yellow mustard seeds
250ml IPA beer
150ml malt vinegar
2 teaspoons soft brown sugar
½ teaspoon salt

Equipment
1 x 500ml preserving jar

Mushroom Ketchup

30g dried porcini mushrooms
20ml vegetable oil
2 Spanish onions, peeled
 and sliced
300g chestnut mushrooms,
 cleaned and quartered
250g button mushrooms,
 cleaned and halved
50ml malt vinegar
1 teaspoon Worcestershire
 sauce
1 teaspoon Dijon mustard
1 teaspoon muscovado sugar
¼ nutmeg, grated
½ teaspoon table salt

Place the dried porcini mushrooms in 200ml of hot water and leave to soak for 1 hour.

Heat the oil in a pan over a medium heat and add the onions. Gently cook the onions for 10 minutes or until they soften and start to brown. Add the chestnut and button mushrooms to the pan and cook for a further 5–10 minutes or until the mushrooms start to colour.

Drain the porcini mushrooms, reserving the soaking liquid. Add the porcini to the pan with the other mushrooms and cook for a further 2 minutes.

Add the remaining ingredients to the pan, including the reserved porcini soaking liquid, and simmer until the liquid has reduced by two-thirds. Transfer the contents of the pan to a blender and process to a smooth purée.

This ketchup will keep for up to one month when stored in an airtight container and kept in the refrigerator.

Devilled Butter

220g butter, softened
1 banana shallot, finely diced
a pinch of fine table salt
1 teaspoon English mustard
¼ bunch tarragon, leaves
 picked and chopped
½ teaspoon cayenne pepper
juice of ½ lemon

Warm 20g of the butter in a small saucepan over a medium heat. Add the diced shallots and salt and, stirring continuously, cook for around 3 minutes or until soft. If necessary, lower the heat to stop the shallots from colouring. Transfer the shallots to paper towels and set aside to drain and cool.

Combine the remaining butter, mustard, tarragon and cayenne pepper in a bowl. Add a squeeze of lemon juice and mix with a fork until well combined. Add the cooked shallots and stir through the butter mixture.

Shape the butter mixture into a log and wrap it tightly in clingfilm, firmly twisting the ends and chill in the refrigerator until needed. The devilled butter will keep for up to two weeks when wrapped in clingfilm and kept in the refrigerator.

Chipshop Curry Sauce

Place a pan over a medium heat and add the oil and butter. Once the butter has melted, add the onion, apple and chilli and cook for 5 minutes or until the onion has softened. Add the curry powder and other spices to the pan and, stirring continuously, cook for 2–3 minutes.

Pour the stock into the pan over the onion mixture and bring to a lively simmer. Leave to cook until the stock has reduced by one-third. Add the cream and continue to reduce the sauce until the sauce is thick enough to coat the back of a spoon.

Pour half the sauce into a blender and process until smooth and transfer to a clean pan. Repeat with the remaining sauce. Finally, whisk the yoghurt into the smooth sauce, add the lime juice and season with salt.

This sauce will keep for up to three days when stored in an airtight container and kept in the refrigerator. Alternatively, it can be frozen for up to one month.

2 teaspoons vegetable oil
10g butter
2 Spanish onions, peeled and sliced
1 cooking apple, peeled, cored and diced
1 red chilli, deseeded and finely chopped
1 tablespoon Madras curry powder
½ teaspoon chilli powder
½ tablespoon ground turmeric
½ teaspoon cumin powder
500ml chicken stock
100ml double cream
25g natural yoghurt
juice of ½ lime
½ teaspoon table salt

Green Sauce

3 salted anchovy fillets
50g flat-leaf parsley, leaves
    picked
25g basil, leaves picked
25g mint, leaves picked
15g capers, drained
zest of 1 lemon
100ml extra-virgin olive oil
1 teaspoon red wine vinegar
1 teaspoon Dijon mustard
½ teaspoon table salt

Place all the ingredients in a blender and process until smooth.
Adjust the seasoning to taste.

Onion, Thyme & Stout Gravy

1 litre beef stock
440ml stout
40g butter
2 teaspoons vegetable oil
4 Spanish onions, peeled
    and sliced
½ teaspoon table salt
15g plain flour
4 thyme sprigs, leaves picked

Place a pan over a high heat, pour in the beef stock and stout and leave to reduce by two-thirds.

Meanwhile, melt the butter and oil in another pan and add the onions and salt. Gently cook the onions for 15 minutes, stirring frequently, until they start to brown. Do not rush cooking the onions; any water in the onions needs to evaporate fully in order for the natural sugars to caramelise. Add the flour and thyme to the pan with the onions and, stirring continuously, cook for a further 2 minutes.

Once reduced, gradually add half the stock to the pan with the onions. Stirring continuously, bring the stock with the onions back up to heat and allow it to thicken. Add the remaining stock to the pan and cook further until the gravy is thick enough to coat the back of a spoon. If the gravy is too thick, add a splash of water. If the gravy is too thin, continue to reduce it for a little longer.

White Butter Sauce

Put the shallots, tarragon and bay leaf in a pan and pour over the vinegar and 100ml of cold water. Place the pan over a medium heat and leave to reduce by two-thirds.

Strain the reduced liquid into a bowl, discarding the shallots, tarragon and bay leaf. Return the liquid to the pan and add the double cream. Place it back over the heat and continue to reduce the sauce for a further 2 minutes.

Take the pan off the heat. Add a handful of the diced butter to the sauce and whisk until fully incorporated. Put the pan back on the heat to get a little warmth back into the sauce, then take it off again and add another handful of butter and whisk again. Repeat until all the butter is emulsified into the sauce.

Add the salt and juice of half the lemon to the sauce. Check the seasoning and adjust by adding a little more lemon juice to taste.

Do not store this sauce in the refrigerator. Like hollandaise sauce, it will split when it becomes too cold.

1 banana shallot, peeled and finely sliced
2 tarragon sprigs
1 bay leaf
100ml white wine vinegar
50ml double cream
400g cold butter, diced
½ teaspoon salt
juice of 1 lemon

Mango Salsa

Place the diced mango in a bowl and then add the lime zest and juice. Add the onion, chilli, coriander and olive oil and mix well. Season with salt and pepper to taste.

1 large ripe mango, peeled and cut into 1cm dice
zest and juice of 1 lime
1 red onion, finely diced
1 red chilli, deseeded and finely chopped
20g coriander, leaves and stalks roughly chopped
2 teaspoons olive oil
salt and freshly ground black pepper

Clockwise from top left:
Hollandaise Sauce (page 258), Onion,
Thyme & Stout Gravy (page 254),
Mushroom Ketchup (page 252), White
Butter Sauce (page 255), Old-School
Mint Sauce (page 250) and Mango Salsa
(page 255)

Hollandaise Sauce

1 shallot, peeled and
finely sliced
20ml white wine
20ml white wine vinegar
5 black peppercorns
a large pinch of table salt
300g butter
3 egg yolks
a pinch of cayenne pepper
½ lemon

Put the shallot, wine, vinegar, peppercorns and salt into a small saucepan and bring to the boil over a medium heat and leave to reduce by half. Remove the pan from the heat and strain the wine and vinegar reduction through a sieve into a metal bowl.

Melt the butter in a microwave until it turns liquid. Pour the golden liquid butter into a small jug, leaving the white fats in the bottom of the microwave container. These can be discarded. Alternatively, heat the butter in a pan over a medium heat, allowing the white fats to separate and sink to the bottom, then pour off the golden liquid butter for using later.

Add the egg yolks to the metal bowl with the slightly cooled wine and vinegar reduction. Whisk vigorously until the mixture is airy and slightly thickened.

Place the metal bowl over a small pan of simmering water and whisk continuously until the sauce is well thickened. You should be able to see drag marks from the whisk in the sauce. The moment that the egg turns from raw to lightly cooked (but not scrambled) is quite a small window of time, so it is important to pay attention as you don't want scrambled eggs.

Remove the metal bowl from the heat and sit it on a damp dish towel for support. Gradually pour in the liquid butter, whisking continuously to incorporate it into the sauce. Add the cayenne pepper and then a squeeze of lemon juice to taste.

Do not store this in the refrigerator as it will split when it becomes too cold.

Clockwise from top:
Caper Mayonnaise (page 260),
Hollandaise Sauce (page 258),
Devilled Butter (page 252)
and Mayonnaise (page 260)

Mayonnaise

MAKES 250ML

2 egg yolks
2 teaspoons white wine vinegar
a pinch of salt
100ml vegetable oil
150ml olive oil
½ teaspoon English mustard
1 tablespoon hot water

Combine the egg yolks, vinegar and salt together in a metal bowl. Place a damp dish towel underneath the bowl for support, then whisk the ingredients together. Slowly pour in both of the oils, whisking continuously and stopping every so often to make sure everything is well combined. Add the mustard and hot water, and continue to whisk until smooth. Taste for seasoning and add a little more salt if necessary.

Caper Mayonnaise

MAKES 200G

75g capers, drained
25g flat-leaf parsley, leaves picked and finely chopped
¼ quantity Mayonnaise (see above)

Crush the capers with a rolling pin and then chop them finely. (Crushing the capers first makes them much easier to chop.) Combine the capers and the chopped parsley, then stir through the mayonnaise. The mayonnaise will keep for up to three days when stored in an airtight container and kept in the refrigerator.

Custard

Whisk together the cornflour, sugar and yolks in a bowl.

Gently heat the milk, cream and vanilla pod in a medium-sized saucepan over a medium heat until just about to simmer, whisking constantly to stop it catching on the bottom and to allow the vanilla seeds to loosen from the pod.

Allow it to sit off the heat for a couple of minutes to infuse with the vanilla and then discard the pod. Bring back to a simmer and slowly pour the liquid over the contents of the bowl, whisking the mix all the time.

Pour the mix back into the saucepan and warm over a low heat until it thickens enough to coat a spoon, stirring all the time with a spatula (do not boil it hard!). Serve it immediately, pouring the biggest portion for yourself.

1 heaped tablespoon cornflour
50g caster sugar
2 large egg yolks
350ml semi-skimmed milk
100ml double cream
½ vanilla pod

Frangipane

Beat the butter, sugar and vanilla seeds together until the butter has turned pale and creamy. Add one egg at a time, whisking until each is fully incorporated before adding another.

Once all the eggs are incorporated, use a large metal spoon to fold in the almonds until well mixed. Use as directed in the recipes.

225g butter, softened
225g caster sugar
1 vanilla pod, deseeded, seeds retained
5 medium-sized eggs
225g ground almonds

THE TEAM

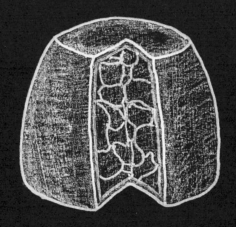

The Team

It's all too common to hear people describe their teams as family but I'm allowed to because it's true. We have 34 chefs and 55 front of house staff across the restaurant, so it's a big family and sometimes we annoy each other, sometimes we tease each other but we always care for each other. I can't talk about every single one of them here, but in the heart of my kitchen team are the seniors who I am going to describe to you: Mark Drummond, Nokx Mbambo, Abdul Turay, Kieron Hibbert, Rosa Di Giacomo, Patrick O'Donnell and Alessandro Giangreco. Their dedication and loyalty over the years continues to astound me; the time they have given to the restaurant collectively is immense and uncommon in a famously transient industry.

So, when I say these people are like family, I genuinely mean it. Mark is my head chef but he is also my brother in everything but blood; he knows everything about me, he knows what to say when I'm upset, he knows how to make me laugh, he lets me know when I'm being unreasonable and I love him for that. He is a talent and will clearly continue making a name for himself and I will support him in that in any way I can.

Nokx has worked with me all over the world, cooking at events and collaboration dinners from Canada and Sweden to Iceland and many other countries. She is the real boss of The Pie Room. We opened it together from the designs to the recipes, and then gradually I knew she was ready to run it day-to-day. She is one of the sweetest people I know and a raw talent in the kitchen. Watching her flourish in her role and in the media has been one of the most rewarding experiences I have had in my career.

Abdul and I have worked together for close to nine years now, he was my witness at my wedding in New Zealand, is affectionately known at times as 'baby rhino' because of the way he charges around the kitchen and he is my rock. I can talk to him about anything, rely on him for anything and if he wanted to, I'd happily work by his side for the rest of my career.

Kieron started with us right from the beginning. He had been working for a friend of mine who was sad to see him go, but asked me to look after him because he knew he had clear promise as a chef. Kieron fitted in from day one. He is smart, driven, skilled and loves winding up Abdul and Nokx (so much so that Mark has now written it into his job description). It's important to encourage people's passions, whatever they are.

Rosa joined our pastry team straight from Italy. She was fiery and tough, with an inspiring work ethic and a love for pastry that was clear for all to see from very early on. She doesn't bat an eyelid at any challenge I throw her way, is absolutely crushing every new dessert menu that we put on and inspires each member of her pastry team to rise to her level and to constantly work on new dishes and development. It's no secret to me that the desserts are one of the strongest parts of our offering at Holborn Dining Room and that all comes from her.

Patrick joined the team three years ago, a charming, polite young chef from Ireland who quickly worked his way up the ranks. He is incredibly mature and responsible for a chef of his age, has a lovely sense of humour and is a natural cook, with a very bright future ahead for him. He also, however, wears the most tasteless socks I have ever seen on a human.

Alessandro was the latest chef to join the senior team. I was well aware that this is a difficult thing to do at first as he was entering a quite tightknit group of people who have worked together for a long time. It was a huge relief to see him fit in so well. He immediately earned everyone's respect through his discipline and drive; he wanted responsibility from the first day and took it on with care and led it to success. Just like the rest of these chefs, he is clearly destined for big things and knows what he wants, and I'll always do all I can to help him achieve it.

This book is for the whole Holborn Dining Room team, the waiters, the bar backs, the porters, the sommeliers ... everyone. I can't thank you enough for everything you have done over the years, for everyone present, for those who have moved on but put love and passion into their work when with us, for all of you, thank you.

INDEX

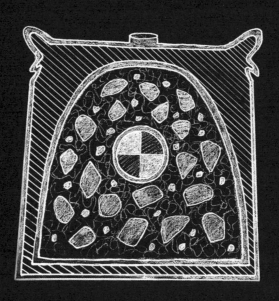

A

apples
  and celeriac remoulade 238
  glazed tart 218
  sauce & pork belly 193
apricots
  and lemon thyme cobblers 217
  pork & sage picnic pie 155

B

Baked Scallops with Green Lentils, Pancetta
  & Red Wine 142
beans minted salad 240
beef
  cheek & kidney suet pudding 156
  keema-spiced cottage pie 171
  Stilton & onion pie 164
  ultimate Wellington 198
beer
  IPA wholegrain mustard 251
  onion, thyme & stout gravy 254
Beet Wellington 110
bone marrow venison suet pie 172
Braised Red Cabbage 232
brioche dough 72
  'nduja stuffed 96
Bubble & Squeak 235
butter
  devilled 252
  white sauce 255

C

cabbage
  braised red 232
  bubble & squeak 235
Caper Mayonnaise 260
carrots
  red onion & hazelnut tatin 123
  slow-roasted & cumin 242
cauliflower curried potato pasties 120
Celeriac & Apple Remoulade 238

cheese
  beef, Stilton & onion pie 164
  Dauphinoise & onion pie 114
  mac 'n' cheese pie 124
  Moroccan chickpea & feta pie 104
  tomato, goats' cheese & onion lattice 109
Cheesy Dauphinoise & Caramelised Onion
  Pie 114
chicken
  coronation pie 206
  mushroom & tarragon pie 148
chickpeas
  Moroccan feta pie 104
  and sweetcorn fritters 241
Chipshop Curry Sauce 253
chocolate panettone & gianduja pudding 214
choux pastry 71
chutneys
  plum & star anise 248
  tomato & red pepper 248
Clapshot 232
classic puff pastry see puff pastry
cod hot & sour curried pie 139
Confit Duck Hash 233
Coronation Chicken Pie 206
cranberries turkey & stuffing pie 152
croquettes leek & white pudding 92
Curried Cauliflower & Potato Pasties 120
custard 261
  rhubarb tart 222

D

decoration 32
desserts see puddings
Devilled Butter 252
Devilled Kidney Vol-au-Vents 95
dough see brioche dough; pastry
duck confit hash 233

E

egg washing 22
eggs
  full English pie 159

Conversion Tables

WEIGHTS

Metric	Imperial
15g	½oz
20g	¾oz
30g	1oz
55g	2oz
85g	3oz
110g	4oz / ¼lb
140g	5oz
170g	6oz
200g	7oz
225g	8oz / ½lb
255g	9oz
285g	10oz
310g	11oz
340g	12oz / ¾lb
370g	13oz
400g	14oz
425g	15oz
450g	6oz / 1lb
1kg	2lb 4oz
1.5kg	3lb 5oz

LIQUIDS

Metric	Imperial
5ml	1 teaspoon
15ml	1 tablespoon or ½fl oz
30ml	2 tablespoons or 1fl oz
150ml	¼ pint or 5fl oz
290ml	½ pint or 10fl oz
425ml	¾ pint or 16fl oz
570ml	1 pint or 20fl oz
1 litre	1¾ pints
1.2 litres	2 pints

LENGTH

Metric	Imperial
5mm	¼ in
1cm	½in
2cm	¾in
2.5cm	1in
5cm	2in
10cm	4in
15cm	6in
20cm	8in
30cm	12in

USEFUL CONVERSIONS

1 tablespoon	= 3 teaspoons
1 level tablespoon	= approx. 15g or ½oz
1 heaped tablespoon	= approx. 30g or 1oz
1 egg	= 55ml / 55g / 1fl oz

OVEN TEMPERATURES

°C	°C Fan	Gas Mark	°F
110°C	90°C Fan	Gas Mark ¼	225°F
120°C	100°C Fan	Gas Mark ½	250°F
140°C	120°C Fan	Gas Mark 1	275°F
150°C	130°C Fan	Gas Mark 2	300°F
160°C	140°C Fan	Gas Mark 3	325°F
180°C	160°C Fan	Gas Mark 4	350°F
190°C	170°C Fan	Gas Mark 5	375°F
200°C	180°C Fan	Gas Mark 6	400°F
220°C	200°C Fan	Gas Mark 7	425°F
230°C	210°C Fan	Gas Mark 8	450°F
240°C	220°C Fan	Gas Mark 9	475°F

About the Author

Calum Franklin is the Executive Chef of Holborn Dining Room, a grand British brasserie in the heart of London. He created The Pie Room at the restaurant in 2018, a kitchen and pie shop designed to reflect the rich history of savoury pastry in Britain across the centuries.

Calum was awarded Hotel Chef of the Year 2019 at the prestigious Catey Awards, and Holborn Dining Room ranked in the top restaurants in the UK at the highly competitive National Restaurant Awards in 2019 for its third consecutive year.

Acknowledgements

A huge thanks to the Absolute Press and Bloomsbury publishing team for bringing me into the fold and putting so, so much into this book. Jon Croft, Meg Boas, Emily North, Marie O'Shepherd, Peter Moffat and Anika Schulze, you are all superstars and it has been a pleasure to work with you from the very first day we spoke about the project.

To John Carey, a friend first and unbelievable photographer second. Thank you for coming on board for this. In my head it was always you, from the first inkling about writing a book, and I'm so happy we got to do this together. Thank you for your beautiful work, the late-night shoots, the flour in your face to get the perfect angle, the Haribo care packages and your friendship.

Thanks so much to the best communication team on the planet: Marie Le Vavasseur, Amelia Harper, Maud Martin and Ashley Grewel at Rosewood London. You all inspire me with your creativity, your hard work and dedication. Marie, honestly, you are the sister that I never had, and I am forever in debt to you and your team for everything you have done for me. You are all Queens.

A huge thank you to all the team at Holborn Dining Room, present and past, for always understanding the goal and giving your all to help us achieve it and for all the help we could ever ask for when shooting the book.

Thank you to Rosewood Hotels for supporting this project, for supporting me when I said I wanted to build a pie room in your stunning hotel, for continuing to support Holborn Dining Room and the dream that we have for it. Special thanks to Michael Bonsor for not only being an incredible boss at all times but also the most stylish man I know and for backing me 100 per cent on this project.

Someone who offered me their time, support and advice at a time I needed it most and never asked for anything back, one of the most generous people I know: Jamie Oliver you are a king, thank you for everything.

Finally, my incredible family. Shenali, you are beautiful in every way and the most supportive wife a man could ask for. You inspire me every day and without you this book would never have happened. Thank you for the feedback, the late nights by my side in the early hours helping me type; thank you for never losing sight of the goal and for always encouraging me to succeed. My mum Lindsay and brothers Jamie and Rory, thank you for everything you have done for me in life and continue to do. I'll never forget how you lifted me up in the hardest of times and I will always be there for you now. This book is for you.

BLOOMSBURY ABSOLUTE
Bloomsbury Publishing Plc
50 Bedford Square, London, WC1B 3DP, UK

BLOOMSBURY, BLOOMSBURY ABSOLUTE, the Diana logo and the
Absolute Press logo are trademarks of Bloomsbury Publishing Plc

First published in Great Britain 2020

A catalogue record for this book is available from the British Library.

Library of Congress Cataloguing-in-Publication data has been
applied for.

HB: 9781472973610
ePub: 9781472973627
ePDF: 9781472973603

2 4 6 8 10 9 7 5 3 1

Printed and bound in China by C&C Offset Printing Co., Ltd.

Bloomsbury Publishing Plc makes every effort to ensure that the
papers used in the manufacture of our books are natural, recyclable
products made from wood grown in well-managed forests. Our
manufacturing processes conform to the environmental regulations
of the country of origin.

To find out more about our authors and books visit
www.bloomsbury.com and sign up for our newsletters.

Publisher
Jon Croft

Commissioning Editor
Meg Boas

Senior Project Editor
Emily North

Art Direction and Design
Peter Moffat and
Marie O'Shepherd

Junior Designer
Anika Schulze

Production Controller
Laura Brodie

Photographer
John Carey

Home Economist
Elaine Byfield

Copyeditor
Lisa Pendreigh

Proofreader
Rachel Malig

Indexer
Zoe Ross

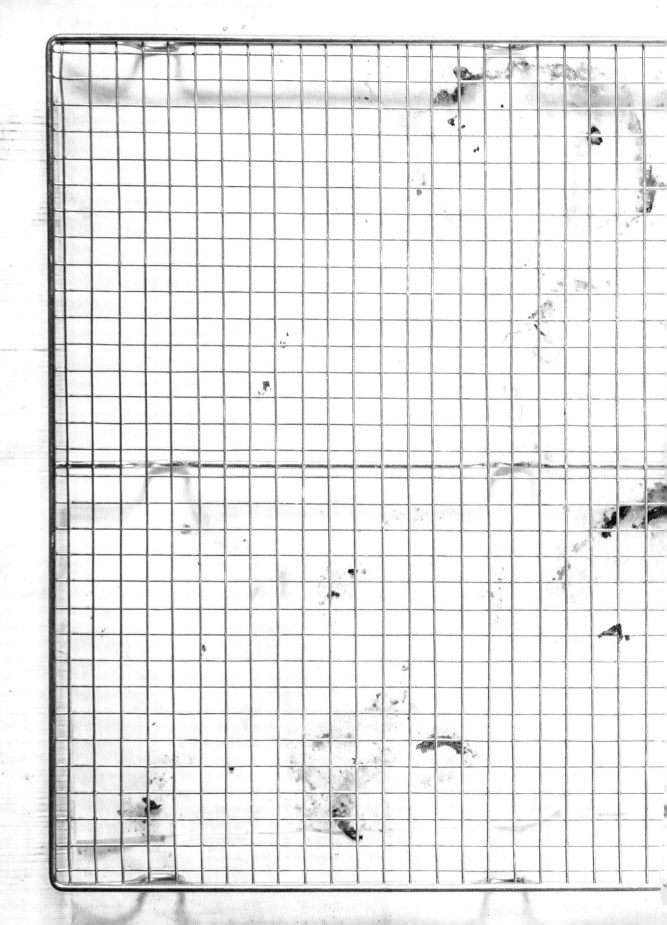